GUITAR EXERCISES

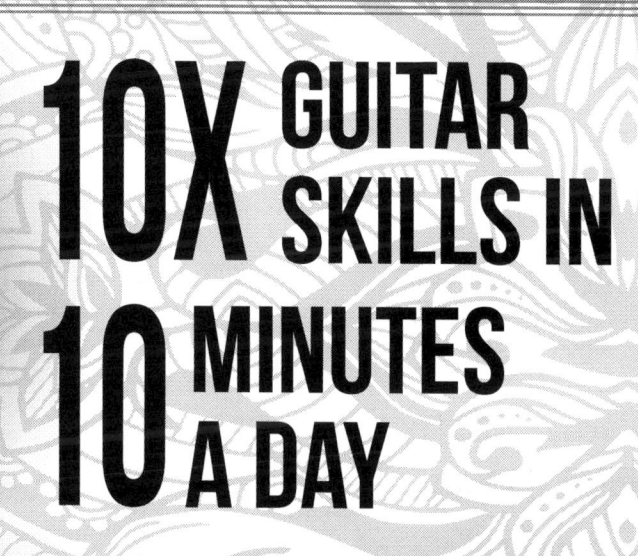

10X GUITAR SKILLS IN 10 MINUTES A DAY

AN ARSENAL OF 100+ EXERCISES FOR ALL AREAS

Guitar Head

GH@theguitarhead.com
www.facebook.com/theguitarhead/

©Copyright 2018 by Guitar Head — All rights reserved.

This document is geared towards providing exact and reliable information in regards to the topic and issue covered. The publication is sold with the idea that the publisher is not required to render accounting, officially permitted, or otherwise, qualified services. If advice is necessary, legal or professional, a practiced individual in the profession should be ordered.

From a Declaration of Principles which was accepted and approved equally by a Committee of the American Bar Association and a Committee of Publishers and Associations.

In no way is it legal to reproduce, duplicate, or transmit any part of this document in either electronic means or in printed format. Recording of this publication is strictly prohibited and any storage of this document is not allowed unless with written permission from the publisher. All rights reserved.

The information provided herein is stated to be truthful and consistent, in that any liability, in terms of inattention or otherwise, by any usage or abuse of any policies, processes, or directions contained within is the solitary and utter responsibility of the recipient reader. Under no circumstances will any legal responsibility or blame be held against the publisher for any reparation, damages, or monetary loss due to the information herein, either directly or indirectly.

Respective authors own all copyrights not held by the publisher.

The information herein is offered for informational purposes solely, and is universal as so. The presentation of the information is without contract or any type of guarantee assurance.

The trademarks that are used are without any consent, and the publication of the trademark is without permission or backing by the trademark owner. All trademarks and brands within this book are for clarifying purposes only and are the owned by the owners themselves, not affiliated with this document.

Disclaimer

Please note the information contained within this document is for educational and entertainment purposes only. Every attempt has been made to provide accurate, up to date and reliable complete information. No warranties of any kind are expressed or implied. Readers acknowledge that the author is not engaging in the rendering of legal and financial, medical or professional advice. The content of this book has been derived from various sources. Please consult a licensed professional before attempting any techniques outline in this book.

By reading this document, the reader agrees that under no circumstances are is the author responsible for any losses, direct or indirect, which are incurred as a result of the use of information contained within this document, including, but not limited to, — errors, omissions, or inaccuracies.

Table of Content

Free Audio Tracks and Bonuses 6

I Can't Read Guitar TABS 9

Chapter #1. How to Use This Book 11
    What's inside? 12
    How do I use it? 13
    The Magic of Every day. 13
    How do I 10x my guitar skills? .14

Chapter #2. The Exercises are too Hard 15
    Getting out of your comfort zone 15

Chapter #3. Before You Start 18
    Pre-Practice Relaxation 18
    String Skip Spider 19
    Eyes Wide Open 20
    Slippery Slope 21
    Post-Practice Stretching 22

Chapter #4. Play Better and Longer 23
    Stir It Up 23
    Burn The Page 25
    Double Shot 25
    Ready Aim Fire 26
    Cracking The Code 27
    Laying The Groundwork 27
    Shifting Logs 28
    Bullets from Nowhere 29
    Close Encounters of the Third Inversion 30
    Trial by Fire 31

Out in The Open 32
Chromatic Legato 32
Crystal Cave. 33
Spicy Neighbours. 34
Attack! 35

Chapter #5. Play Faster and Accurately 36
Chromasweep 37
The Ascent. 38
The Descent 38
Fire in The Cabin 39
Fire in The Cockpit 40
Eerie Sweeps 40
Three by Five 41
Just Tap Water for Me 42
Peckin' Around 43
Ripples in The Water 44
Seventh Seal. 45
Sliding Over Steps 45
String Skip Legato 46
I'll Get a Lift 47
Trail Mix. 48

Chapter #6. Tame Your Picking Hand 50
Starting The Engine 51
Pima Puma 52
The Hen's Walk 52
Three Feet Under 53
Bottom Up 53
To The Sun and Back 54
Jump The Rope. 54
Economy 101 55
Middle Ground 55
Soaring Waves 56

Chapter #7. Play Legendary Solos 57
Yin and Yang 58
Just A Couple 58
Rainy Morning 59
Sprints 60
Car Chase 60
Just Perfect 61

    Cow Lick..61
    Enclosing Beasts...62
    Passing By..63
    Move Those Boxes..63
    Internal Triads...64
    Three Trees..65
    The Leap..66
    That Escalated Quickly..67
    Climbing Back Up..68

Chapter #8. Master Chords & Arpeggio.........................69
    Through Stained Glass..69
    Raising The Barre..70
    Chilling at Nine..71
    Fresh Moves...71
    Suspension Bridge...72
    Sleepy Time..72
    Asking Questions...73
    A Drop in The Bucket...73
    Wait, I'm Confused...74
    Ghostly Rhythms..74

Chapter #9. A Few Fun Exercises...............................75
    Vibin' In Detroit..75
    Impending Doom...76
    Chunky Riff...77
    Picking Drill..77
    Oh, I Wonder..78

Until Next Time!...81

Free Audio Tracks and Bonuses

Congratulations on selecting a Guitar Head book. If it's your first time getting one of our books, I want to welcome you to our little world.

At Guitar Head, our mission is *to help you find a purpose with guitar so you can find happiness and identity in it.*

This mission comes from the special bond I share with my guitar. My guitar has been by my side since I was 12. I started playing as a way to look cool in school but it soon grew to be something much bigger than that. It gave me something to work on every day, it gave me excitement in life, it gave me access to some very talented people and the best thing of all – it gave me an identity which I wear proudly – the identity of a guitarist!

And now, with Guitar Head – I want to help you create the same relationship with the guitar.

I've seen far too many guitarists – pros and beginners alike – failing to create a connection with the guitar. They concentrate only on the mechanics of playing guitar – playing faster, playing more songs, playing techniques, getting your fingers to do that, do this……… without really taking the time to build a relationship with the instrument.

With Guitar Head, I want to change things around! I want to help you build a relationship with the guitar. I want to make guitar your partner through the ups and downs of life – not just a musical instrument that you can play. Something that can give you happiness and energy, something that can be your escape during dark times, something that will give you access to talented people, something that can give you all the confidence in the world.

And how do you do that? – You build a relationship with your guitar. You find a strong purpose with music and guitar! That's what Guitar Head is all about. That's what we do and that's what we want to help you do.

Now, I'll need more than half a page to help you find your purpose and relationship with the guitar. Hence, let's continue this discussion through email. This section was intended only to give you a brief introduction of what we stand for and how we can help you on your guitar journey.

Download any of the bonuses below to become an email subscriber and we can continue our conversation there. I'll see you in your inbox!

Oh, one more thing! You can also get the below bonuses for free when you sign up to be a part of Guitar Head. They're tools that'll help your guitar journey and help you use this book the way it was intended to be used. Go get your hands on it before you start the book – you don't want to stop the book midway, download the bonuses and come back.

Here is a list of bonuses that you get with this book:

1. **Audio Tracks:** The audio tracks provided with this book are an integral part of the content. It ensures that you are playing the charts and chords the way it was intended to be played.

2. **A Free Book:** Guitar mastery is all about nailing those small elements and avoiding mistakes. In this book, I explain 25 such mistakes and provide ways to avoid them.

3. **Access to a private community of passionate guitarists:** Being around like-minded people is the first step in being successful at anything. The Guitar Head community is full of passionate guitarists who help each other excel. When you buy a Guitar Head book, you

automatically become a part of this amazing community of people who are willing to listen to your music, answer your questions or talk anything guitar.

4. **Weekly Guitar Lessons:** Every Saturday – you'll receive a fresh piece of content delivered right to your inbox. The lessons range from things like *How to buy your first guitar* to *Tabs to your favorite songs*.

You can follow the below link to become a subscriber and get your hands on all the above bonuses:

www.theguitarhead.com/bonus

P.S. Write to support@theguitarhead.com if you need help downloading the bonuses.

I Can't Read Guitar TABS

Learning guitar without learning to read tabs is very much like crossing a busy road — blindfolded!

What do you do when you can't read? – You learn the alphabets.

What do you do when you can't count? – You learn the numbers.

What do you do when you can't read tabs? – You leave an offensive 1-star review on the book and you'll wake up the next day having complete knowledge on how to read tabs! (I'm just kidding – but disturbingly, that's what a few reviewers did!)

I understand if you are a beginner and can't read tabs; every person who can play the guitar has gone through that, including me. But the solution is not to get angry at the author and trash him in the review section. That's like saying "I want to learn to drive but I won't learn to read the street signs, I'll throw a stone at a cop instead!"

I feel sad for such people! They are missing out on such vital information! Learning to read guitar tabs won't take more than 30 minutes of your time and is very essential skill to have if you are learning guitar! Every guitar site, video or book on the internet communicates through written tabs and it is one of the first steps I teach in my students and in my book "Guitar for Beginners".

So, if you don't know to read tabs, I urge you to learn it before you take another step into the book. To make it easier for you, I wrote a whole book dedicated to reading tabs! It will teach you everything you need to know about reading tabs! And what's better – I'm giving it away for free!

You can get it here for free: *www.theguitarhead.com/tabs*

I want the paperback version:

If you want the paperback version of the book, you can get it on my website.

With your new-found tab reading skills and the free audio tracks that come with this book, I can already see you crushing the licks inside! Have fun!

Chapter #1

How to Use This Book

(Do not skip this)

Guitar exercises are something many guitarists don't enjoy as much as jamming to their favorite songs. I don't blame them; guitar exercises are often the boring, routine 1-2-3 exercises that you have been doing from the very first day you picked up a guitar. This book is here to change that — to make guitar exercises fun and compelling. With over 110 different FUN exercises, you will never be bored again.

Guitar exercises are crucial. They are specific and targeted at certain areas. For the sake of this explanation, let's say your bending skills are below average. While you can find a song with a lot of bending, the writer surely didn't write the song to help you improve your skills. It was meant to sound as good as possible. This is where depending on songs to improve your skills hits a stone wall. On the flip side, if you decide to increase the strength of your fingers by following a few exercises mentioned in this book, you will be way ahead of what you can expect from a song. You see, exercises are like missiles; you can enter the exact coordinates and the missile will go straight to the target in the most efficient way.

Here are some general tips and "how-to knowledge" to help you go through the book with ease.

What's inside?

This book contains 75 title exercises broken down into multiple smaller exercises, which brings us to around 110 exercises in total. Each exercise is my baby and has been built with specific areas in mind. That would explain the elaborate table of contents page giving importance to each exercise. Each exercise is special and, hence, given a unique name and tag. Special care has been taken to make sure that each exercise is unique and is to be found only this book.

The exercises in the book are arranged in an ascending order of their difficulty. Each exercise also contains a tag narrating the techniques involved, difficulty level, and category. This should make it easier for you to find the right type of exercise exactly when you need it.

The book is designed to entertain the beginners and the pros alike. As each exercise has its own tag, you may judge it before you give it a shot and make sure that the exercise is of your skill level. The skill level mentioned is a general indicator of difficulty and should not be considered for skipping exercises. An exercise that may seem advanced to you may, in actuality, be an intermediate exercise. So, I urge you to give each exercise a shot, even if you know for a fact that it's beyond your skill level.

I would also like to bring to your attention the fact that this book is purely an exercise book. I will not be teaching the various techniques involved. If you are interested in learning more on the techniques involved, feel free to email me at *GH@theguitarhead.com*. I would love to create more content for you.

You will not find huge descriptions for each exercise to bulk up the pages. The book is true to its name and will offer quality exercises along with necessary descriptions.

How do I use it?

A gym is a perfect metaphor for this book. The book contains various exercises such as bench press, chest press, barbell curl etc. Each exercise has been aimed at specific areas such as strength, stamina, speed, dexterity instead of chest, biceps or triceps. What you should do is repeat each exercise as many times as possible to build up each area. The more you can repeat, the better you get. If you feel you need to improve on your guitar speed, simply open up the speed section in the book and practice the exercises until you get your desired result.

The Magic of Every day

Look for magic in your daily routine.

– Lou Barlow

What you concentrate on, on a regular basis, grows. That's the mantra of every successful person out there. The same goes with guitar; practice every day and you will soon see results you never dreamed possible. Allow me to explain.

To bring my point out, let me introduce two imaginary characters — Richard and Ralph. Both love to play the guitar and both have regular jobs and families that keep them hopping all the time. To bring guitar into their routine, both come up with an action plan. Richard decides to play guitar for half an hour every day, as that's all the time he can spare in a working day. Ralph, on the other hand, decides to play guitar every weekend for hours at a time.

Who do you think will become a better guitarist in the long run? If your guess was Richard, you are right!

Playing guitar is a skill that needs commitment and constant attention. It does not matter if you can only afford to spend 10 minutes a day on your guitar, you will be better than a person spending hours all at once when he finds time. Ten minutes every day is better than 2 hours on the weekend.

This is the difference I intend on making through this book. It does not matter if you are a professional guitarist or a beginner playing guitar as a hobby. If you are serious about this wonderful instrument, you should play at least 10 minutes every day.

You may surely practice more than 10 minutes a day, but I would like to keep our topic of discussion at 10 minutes to make sure that you get in the bare minimum.

How do I 10x my guitar skills?

Play every day! That's the mantra when it comes to guitar skills. Let's say you play half an hour a day; at least 10 minutes of the 30 minutes should be solely dedicated to guitar exercises.

Steve Vai, one of the greatest guitarists of all time, still does guitar exercises for an hour before he starts his practice session. He has made it a routine to work his fingers for an hour before his practice sessions. This is one of my objective through this book – to give you your very own personalised exercise routine.

Just like you would work out at a gym, pick out the area you would like to target each day and work your fingers to become a better guitarist. You may have a strength day, speed day, picking hand day, etc.

Follow a consistent routine for enough time and you will soon start noticing those gains! You will notice drastic improvements in your abilities as a guitarist.

Chapter #2

The Exercises are too Hard

I've had many people reach out to me saying the exercises in the book are too hard and I've had a few people lash out at me in the review section saying the exercises are too hard, the exercises don't make sense, don't bother with this book etc. Therefore I decided to have an entire chapter just to address this issue.

Now, I agree, some of the exercises inside the book might seem a little hard for a person starting out. But how is that a bad thing?

Getting out of your comfort zone

*Everything you ever wanted
is one step outside your comfort zone!*

Pushing yourself to play things that are out of you level of comfort is how you progress with the guitar and in life. You can't expect to make considerable progress with the guitar if you only play things that you are comfortable with.

This book has NOT been designed to be completed in a day, rather, I see it as a companion throughout your guitar journey. From the very start of your journey to the day you feel you've covered a lot of ground on the fretboard – I want this book to be by your side! You can see the benefits of the book coming months and years from now. Trust me when I say this – there are a few exercises in this book that even I can't play without breaking a sweat, and *I wrote the book!*

If you are a beginner, I suggest you start with the exercises with the beginner tag and progress your way to the intermediate as you advance in your guitar journey! Surely you won't be bumping up levels today or tomorrow – it is a gradual process!

Break it down

While I have tried to break down all the exercises into bite-sized pieces that you can repeat over and over, if at any point you find an exercise difficult to play in one go, I would advise that you break it down into smaller bits and practice the bits over and over. You need not play the whole section in one shot. You will receive the same benefits if you do the exercise in one go or in pieces. The objective here is to make progress in improving on this skill and to have fun.

DO NOT try to play the whole exercise in one shot. Learn a bite sized part of the lick and practice it over and over until you feel you are making progress.

I hope you understand my mentality around this book. It is meant to be challenging, it is meant to push you beyond your limits, it is meant to be "not easy"!

I'm also working on a complete beginner's book for exercises, which should be out soon. So, stay tuned for that.

Take your time

This book contains around 110 exercises. While it could be exciting to finish all of them in one go, I would advise against it. First, the aim of the book is to build your different skill sets, such as accuracy, strength, stamina, etc. This requires a lot of repetition and practicing the same riff over and over again, until you feel the stretch in your hands. It is very much like working out in a gym — you do not want to cover all the equipment in one day. Ideally, what you should be doing is covering a few pieces of equipment, but in an organized and effective manner. That is how I want you to look at this book, as a group of equipment on which you should work systematically to see results.

Second, it can be very frustrating going through a lot of exercises in one shot. You have been warned, do not do that! I know, as when I was in the editing phase of the book, I had to play over all the exercises. While it is fun to play individual exercises, it can be very frustrating to play multiple ones at a time. The book is yours now and you can spend all the time you want with it. I would advise you to go through it slow and steady.

Chapter #3

Before You Start

My guitar is not a thing. It is an extension of myself. It is who I am.

– Joan Jett

Just like you would do in a gym, stretches and warmups are essential to a good practice session with the guitar. Here are a few warmups and general stretches before we get into the meat of the matter.

Pre-Practice Relaxation

The first step to ensure a productive practice session is preparing the body to undertake the physical strains inherent to all guitar techniques. Contrary to popular belief, extensive stretching before playing might actually be counterproductive, rendering the still cold muscles and tendons weaker and more vulnerable to damage.

The best strategy is to gently warm-up your upper body, and eliminate all tension from your joints. Here are some steps you can follow to do so:

A

The neck and shoulder joints are at the core of proper posture and technique, overlooked stress in that area will have repercussions up to the tips of your fingers.

Start by standing up, arms loose and close to your body, then start by rolling your shoulders forward while gently opening and closing your hand for a minute; repeat, this time rolling your shoulders backwards.

B

Now slowly rotate your head in a clockwise and anti-clockwise motion, 30 seconds each.

C

Still standing up with your arms close to your body, raise your forearms to form a 90-degree angle at your elbows. While keeping your grip loose and hand straight, bend your wrist upwards and then back down for a minute; repeat, this time bending your wrist downwards.

This will warm-up the tendons in your forearm, the same tendons controlling the motion in your fingers.

String Skip Spider

Category: Fretting & Picking Hand
Techniques: String Skipping, Alternate Picking

(For anyone who skipped the initial pages of the book, I am providing free audio tracks that go along with the licks in this book, please refer the initial pages of this book to find out how you can get them)

Description: Spider exercises aim to work every finger in various combinations, but this one presents a little string skipping twist. It's a rarely encountered movement for the picking hand, and executing it accurately requires some adjustment time.

Economy of motion is paramount as always, however, to make the most out of the task, keep all pitches fretted for as long as you can, therefore working your stamina as well as your dexterity.

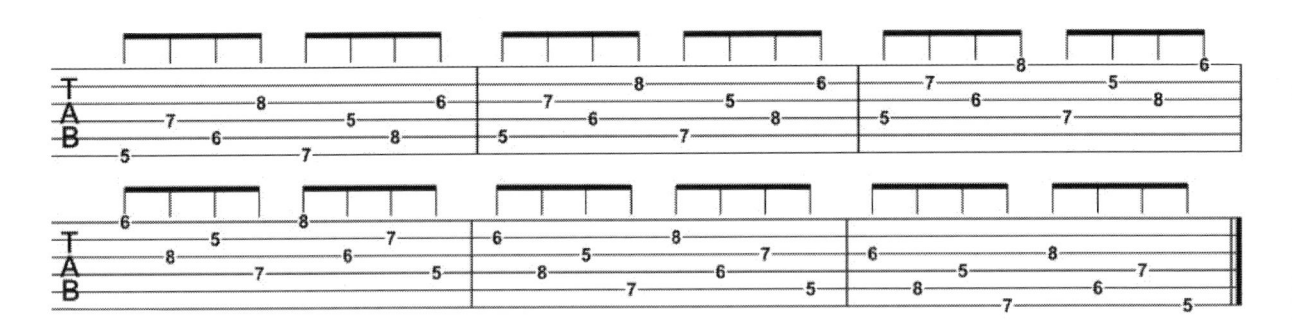

Eyes Wide Open

Category: Fretting & Picking Hand
Techniques: Finger Stretching, Sweep Picking/Fingerstyle

Description: Static effort can bear the same results as dynamic movement in a warmup routine. The wide chord voicings presented in this exercise promote blood flow in the fretting hand, while requiring the elimination of any excess stress or tension to be maintained.

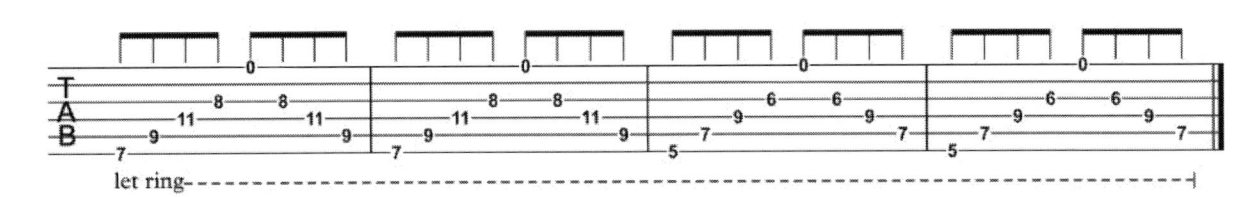

Slippery Slope

Category: Fretting Hand
Techniques: Legato

Description: A simple hammer-on/pull-off drill working all fingers. Proper legato execution requires a combination of raw strength and fine movement coordination, rendering it an excellent device to initiate a productive practice session.

A

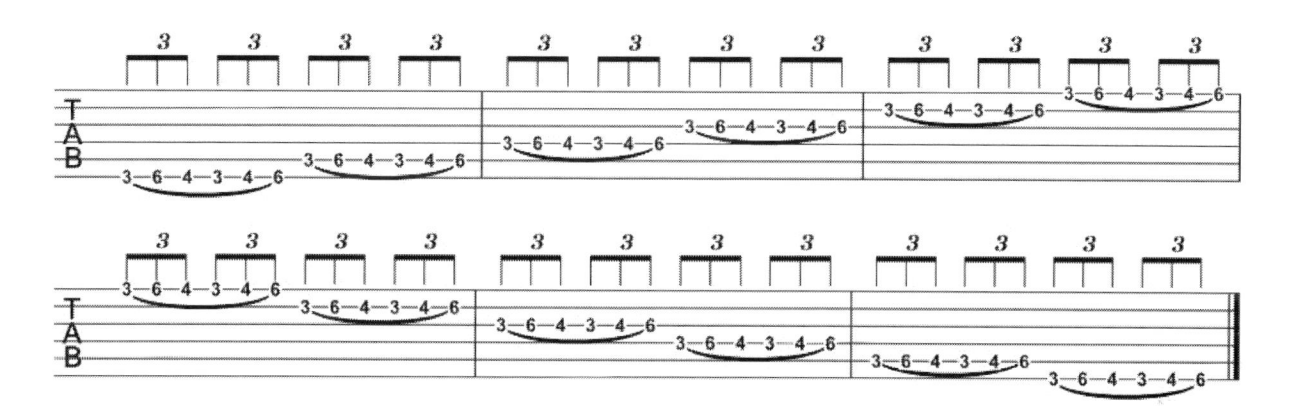

B

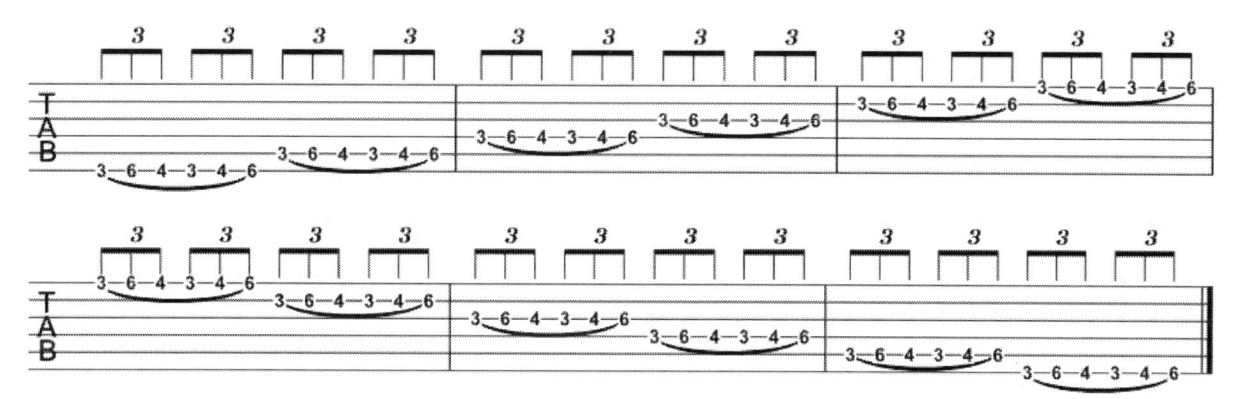

Post-Practice Stretching

This section consists of a few basic stretches you would want to do after your productive practice session is complete. You can use some stretching routines to wind down and facilitate your recovery.

A

While standing up, raise your arms as far up as you can and maintain this position for ten seconds; now repeat, this time trying to touch your toes.

B

Stand in front of a wall and place your right palm on its surface with your fingers pointing up, keeping the arm straight, maintain for five seconds and repeat with your fingers pointing down; repeat for the other arm.

C

Now turn to your side and raise your arm to shoulder's height, placing your palm on the wall.

Get your body closer to the wall by slowly sliding your arm back, get as close to the wall as you can and hold for ten seconds; repeat with the other arm.

Chapter #4

Play Better and Longer

I don't need to speak; I play the guitar!

— Joe Perry

Have you ever seen legendary guitarists play for hours together for thousands of people without breaking a sweat? They gig for hours together without thinking about it. This is because they've built the stamina to play for hours and the strength to keep that bend ringing.

This is what we will learn in this chapter – increasing your finger strength and stamina. I have created multiple exercises to target your finger muscles. There is going to be a lot of heavy lifting and legato in this chapter.

Let's get right into it, shall we?

Stir It Up

Category: Fretting Hand
Level: Beginner
Techniques: Legato

GUITAR EXERCISES

Description: The premise of this exercise is fairly simple: targeting all possible finger combinations in a legato setting. Assigning a finger to each fret, ascend using hammer-ons and descend using pull-offs. Beware of the last combination as ring and pinky fingers are a weak combo, bring the metronome down if necessary.

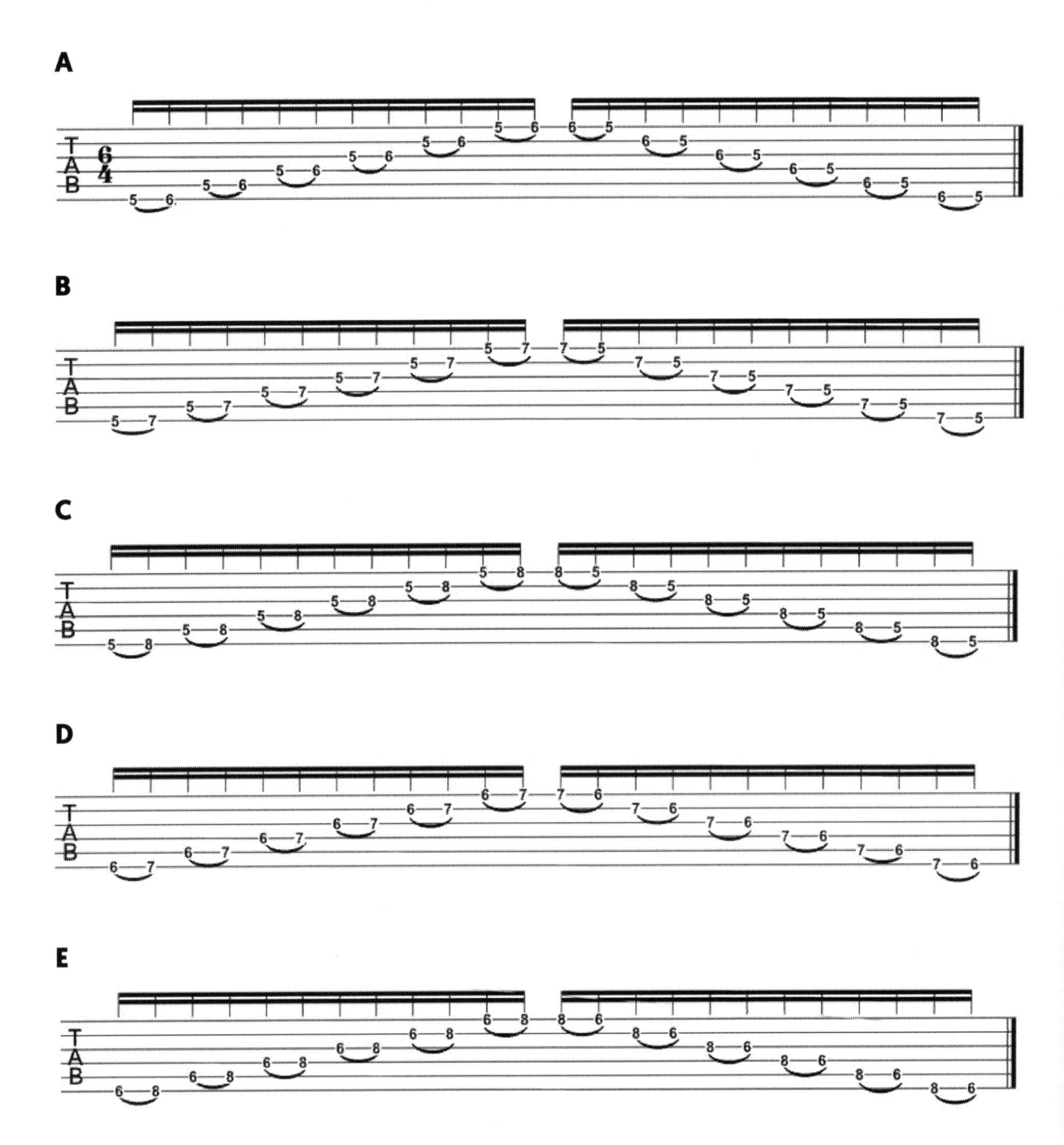

A

```
6/4
-------------------------------------------------------------
-------------------------------------------------------------
-------------------------------------------------------------
-------------------------------------------------------------
-----------------------------------5-6--6-5------------------
-----------------------------5-6------------6-5--------------
-----------------------5-6--------------------6-5------------
-----------------5-6------------------------------6-5--------
-5-6---------------------------------------------------6-5---
```

B

```
-------------------------------5-7--7-5----------------------
-------------------------5-7------------7-5------------------
-------------------5-7------------------------7-5------------
-------------5-7--------------------------------7-5----------
-5-7----------------------------------------------7-5--------
```

C

```
-------------------------------5-8--8-5----------------------
-------------------------5-8------------8-5------------------
-------------------5-8------------------------8-5------------
-------------5-8--------------------------------8-5----------
-5-8----------------------------------------------8-5--------
```

D

```
-------------------------------6-7--7-6----------------------
-------------------------6-7------------7-6------------------
-------------------6-7------------------------7-6------------
-------------6-7--------------------------------7-6----------
-6-7----------------------------------------------7-6--------
```

E

```
-------------------------------6-8--8-6----------------------
-------------------------6-8------------8-6------------------
-------------------6-8------------------------8-6------------
-------------6-8--------------------------------8-6----------
-6-8----------------------------------------------8-6--------
```

24

F

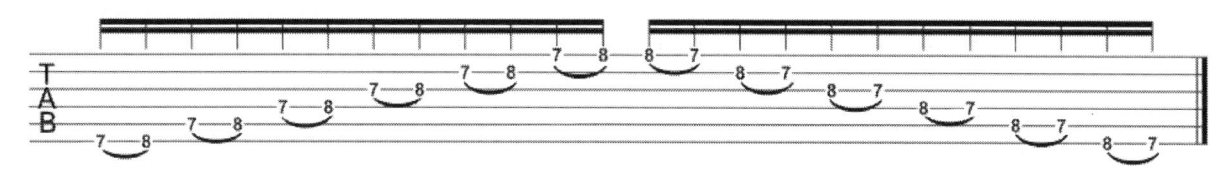

Burn The Page

> **Category: Fretting & Picking Hand**
> **Level: Beginner**
> **Techniques: Finger Roll, Alternate Picking**

Description: A tasty lick straight out of the arsenal of the best hard rock soloists of the 70s. It's an E Minor Pentatonic with some extra chromatic flare. To be played with an alternate picking style, emphasising the initial note of the pattern. Developing the finger roll necessary to consecutively play the same fret on two adjacent strings might take some time, take it slow at first and you'll be cranking that metronome in no time.

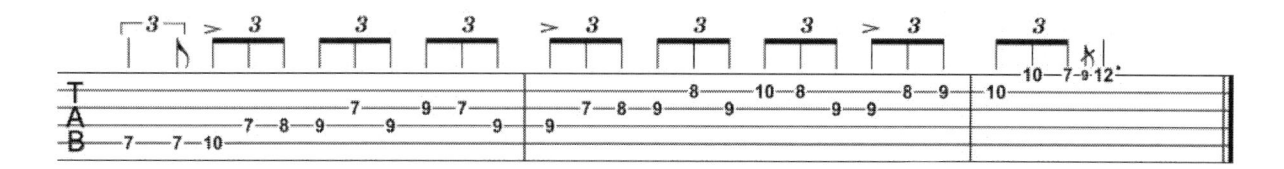

Double Shot

> **Category: Fretting & Picking Hand**
> **Level: Beginner**
> **Techniques: Alternate Picking, Finger Stretching**

Description: A three note per string G Major scalar run where every pitch is repeated twice; this allows the player to focus on economy of motion in the fretting hand while monitoring tension in the picking hand. Ensure adequate articulation of all notes and even dynamics throughout the pattern. Keep in mind that slow tempos bear as much challenge as the faster ones, as you will have to maintain a stretched position for longer.

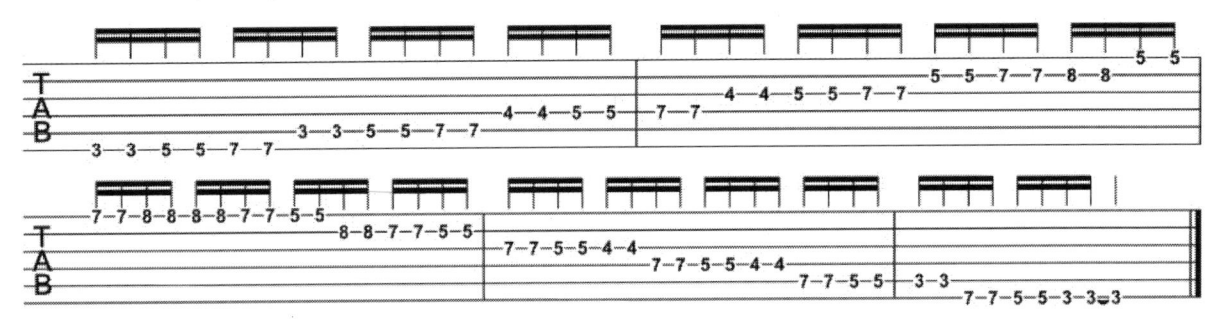

Ready Aim Fire

Category: Fretting Hand
Level: Beginner
Techniques: Bending

Description: Bending strings can be a strenuous activity on the fingers, it stresses the wrist as well as the individual fingers and their skin. This exercise targets both pitch accuracy and endurance with a scalar pattern where the next diatonic pitch is reached by bending rather than fretting. Try it out with every finger, and make sure that the twisting motion comes from the rotation of the wrist, rather than vertical movement of the fingers themselves.

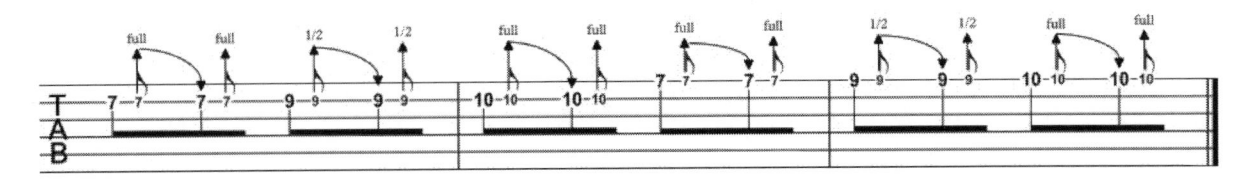

Cracking The Code

Category: Fretting Hand
Level: Beginner
Techniques: Legato

Description: In this legato routine the first finger acts as a pivot for the whole pattern, keep your index in place and let the note ring with confidence and uniformity throughout the exercise.

The pull-off motion of the third and fourth finger will require some dedicated work before seeing satisfactory results, just make sure not to strain your tendons as this is a delicate movement.

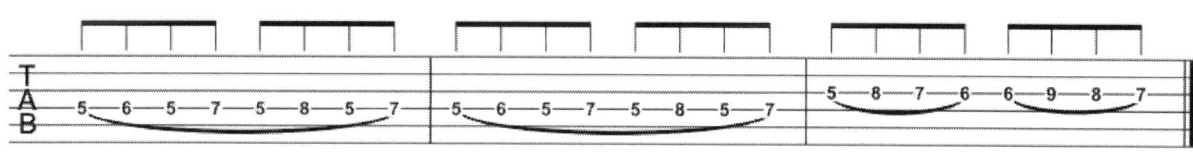

A

```
T|--5--6--5--7--5--8--5--7--|--5--6--5--7--5--8--5--7--|--5--8--7--6--6--9--8--7--|
A|
B|
```

B

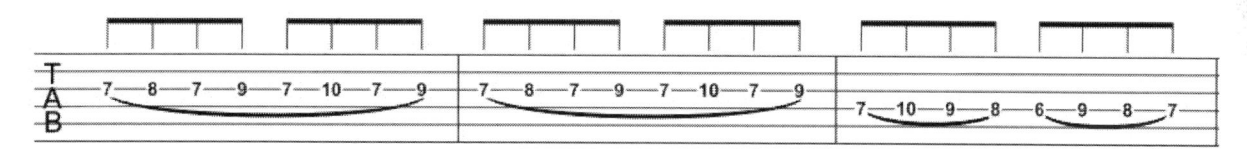

```
T|--7--8--7--9--7--10--7--9--|--7--8--7--9--7--10--7--9--|--7--10--9--8--6--9--8--7--|
A|
B|
```

Laying The Groundwork

Category: Fretting Hand
Level: Intermediate
Techniques: Legato

Description: As simple as it gets. This exercise targets the development of hammer-ons and pull-offs through scalar application. Starting the pattern on the 3rd and 4th degrees of the major scale allows for the exploration of every finger combination you could encounter within its modes. There are a few unusual stretches lurking in the lick, you might want to be cautious!

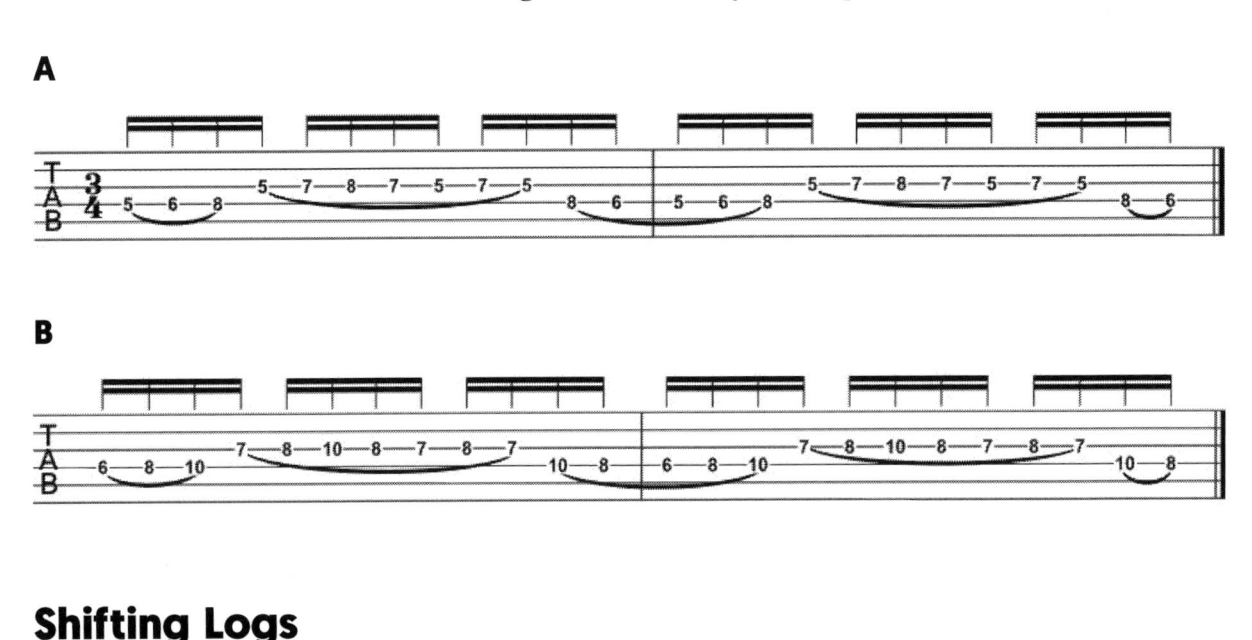

A

```
3/4  5—6—8—5—7—8—7—5—7—5—8—6—5—6—8—5—7—8—7—5—7—5—8—6
```

B

```
6—8—10—7—8—10—8—7—8—7—10—8—6—8—10—7—8—10—8—7—8—7—10—8
```

Shifting Logs

Category: Fretting & Picking Hand
Level: Intermediate
Techniques: Alternate Picking, Finger Stretching

Description: This line presents a sequence of three note per string scalar patterns, but these are now moving horizontally rather than vertically. The position shift can be challenging at higher tempos, make sure to clearly outline the motion and not to lose alternation in the picking hand.

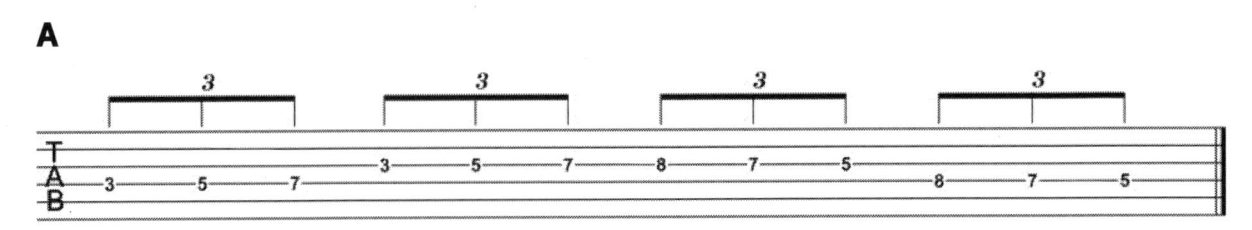

A

```
3—5—7—3—5—7—8—7—5—8—7—5
```

B

```
         3              3               3              3
T|--5--7--8-------5--7--8------10--8--7-------------10--8--7--|
A|-----------------------------------------------------------|
B|-----------------------------------------------------------|
```

C

```
         3              3               3              3
T|--7--8--10------7--8--10-----10--12--10--8-------12--10--8--|
A|------------------------------------------------------------|
B|------------------------------------------------------------|
```

D

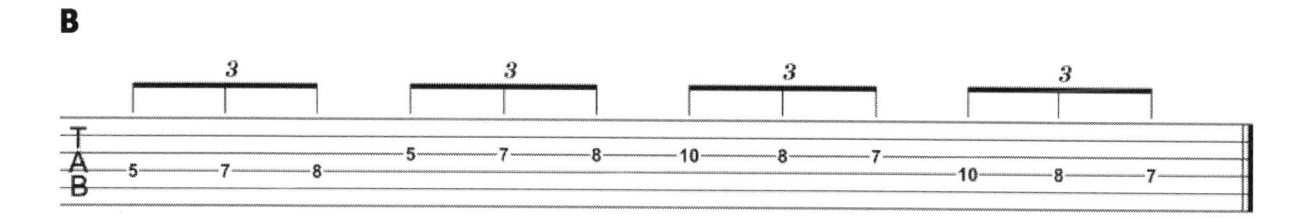

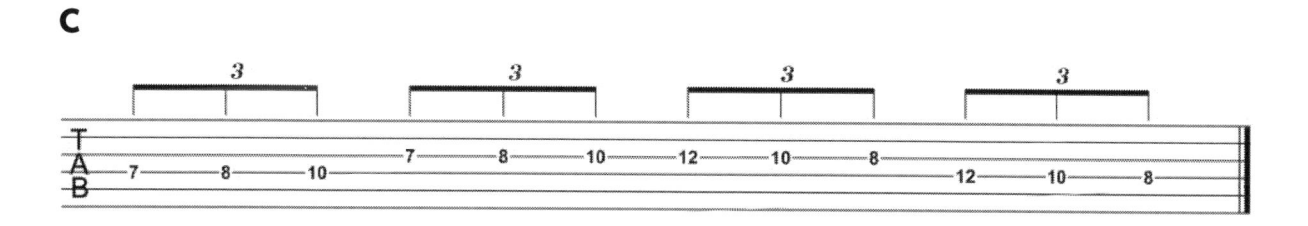

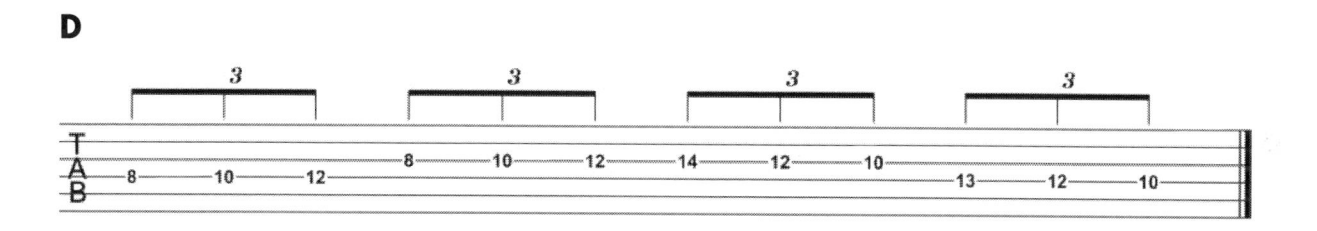

```
         3              3               3              3
T|--8--10--12-----8--10--12----12--14--12--10------13--12--10-|
A|------------------------------------------------------------|
B|------------------------------------------------------------|
```

Bullets from Nowhere

Category: Fretting Hand
Level: Intermediate
Techniques: Hammer-ons from Nowhere

Description: This exercise addresses finger strength through the technique of "hammer-ons from nowhere". Throw your pick away as your left hand will be doing all of the work this time, attack each note with a tapping motion, this will strengthen your tendons and improve their response time. It also works great for finger accuracy. Try out different finger combinations!

GUITAR EXERCISES

A

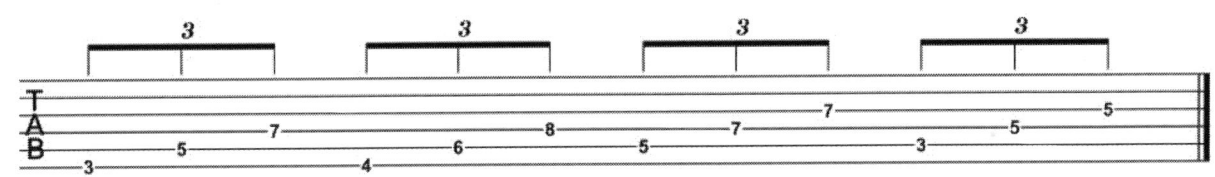

```
T|-------------------------------7-------------------5---|
A|-----5-----7-----------8-----7-----------5---------|
B|-3---------------6---5-----------------3-----------|
          (triplets: 3, 3, 3, 3)
```

B

```
T|---------8-----------8-----------9-----------9-----|
A|-----6-----------6-----------7-----------7---------|
B|-4---------------4-----5-----------------5---------|
          (triplets: 3, 3, 3, 3)
```

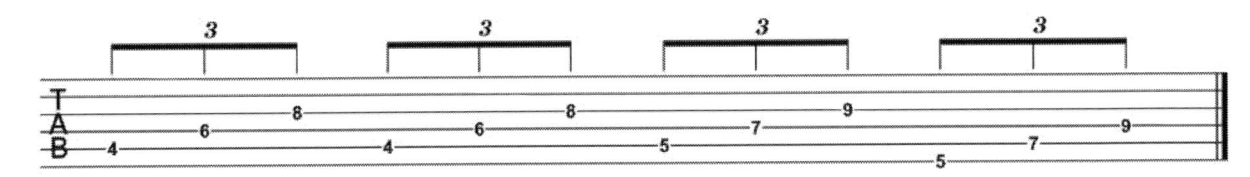

C

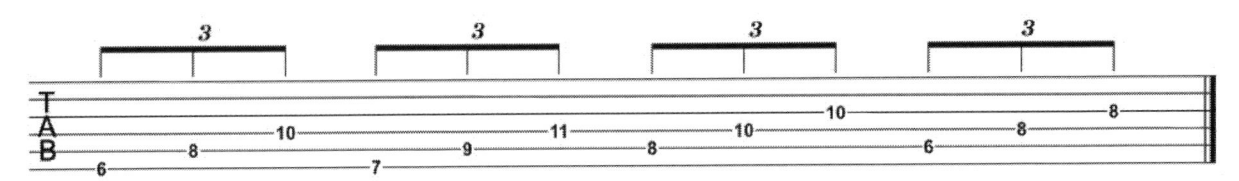

```
T|---------10----------11----10----10----------8-----8|
A|-----8-----------9-------8-----------6-----------|
B|-6---------------7-----------------------------------|
          (triplets: 3, 3, 3, 3)
```

D

```
T|-----11----------11----12----------12----|
A|-9-------9-----------10-------10-------|
B|-7---------7-----8-----------8----------|
          (triplets: 3, 3, 3, 3)
```

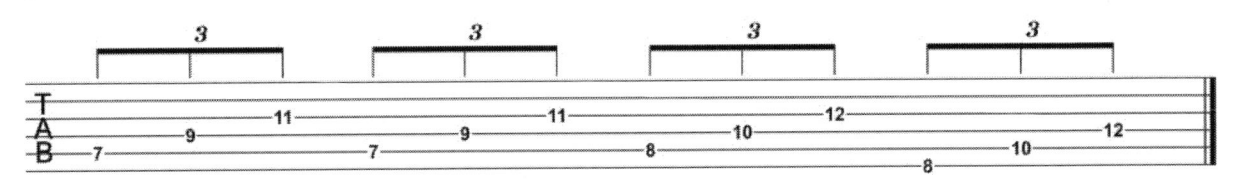

Close Encounters of the Third Inversion

Category: Fretting & Picking Hand
Level: Intermediate
Techniques: Alternate Picking, Position Shifting

Description: A Maj 7th arpeggio spanning three octaves, ascending and descending without losing consistency is a feat in resistance. Economy of motion is the key here, maintain a steady picking pattern while keeping your fingers as close as possible to the fretboard, smoothly shifting your fretting hand between positions. Try breaking it up into bite-sized pieces if you are having trouble nailing it in one go.

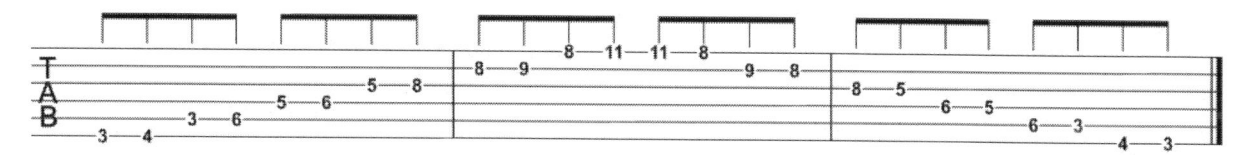

```
T|-------------------------------------8--11--11--8-------------------------------|
A|---------------5--8------------8--9------------9--8----8--5---------------------|
B|-3--4--3--6--5-------------------------------------------6--5---6--5---4--3-----|
```

Trial by Fire

Category: Fretting & Picking Hand
Level: Intermediate
Techniques: Alternate Picking

Description: This neo-classical styled line is as simple as unforgiving, be aware of the proper articulation of each note, and the dynamics between the open string and the fretted pitches. This has to be one of my favorite riffs form this section. Just learn the frets involved and you can noodle away on any string!

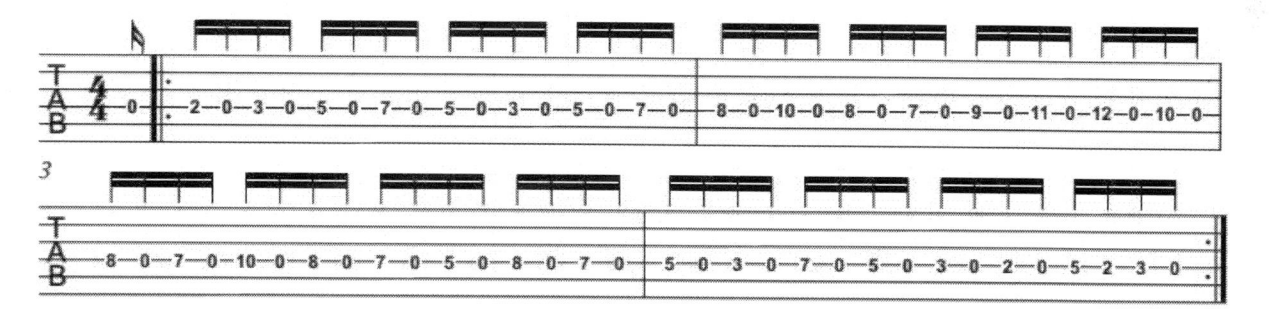

```
T|-0--2-0-3-0-5-0-7-0-5-0-3-0-5-0-7-0--8-0-10-0-8-0-7-0-9-0-11-0-12-0-10-0-|
A|-------------------------------------------------------------------------|
B|-------------------------------------------------------------------------|

T|-8-0-7-0-10-0-8-0-7-0-5-0-8-0-7-0--5-0-3-0-7-0-5-0-3-0-2-0-5-2-3-0-|
```

Out in The Open

Category: Fretting & Picking Hand
Level: Intermediate
Techniques: Downpicking, Economy Picking, Legato

Description: A melodic riff revolving around open chord positions. The first two bars require a mix of downpicking and economy picking to be performed, and the last two bars provide a rest for the picking hand, but call for the employment of hammer-ons and pull-offs involving open strings, so be careful!

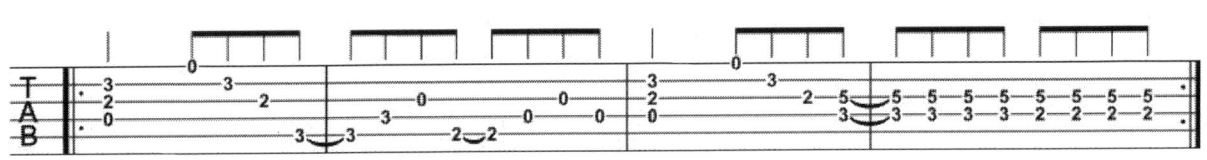

A

B

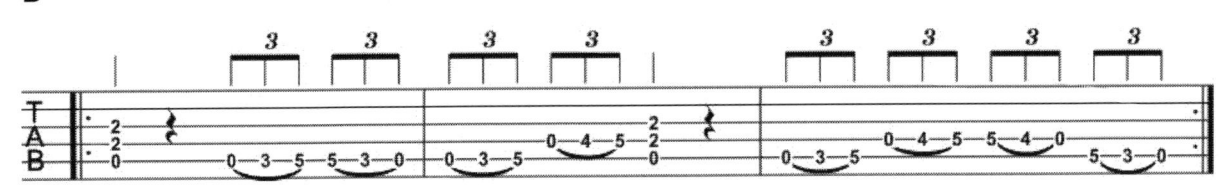

Chromatic Legato

Category: Fretting Hand
Level: Advanced
Techniques: Legato, Finger Stretching

Chapter #4. Play Better and Longer

Description: Hammer-on and pull-off workout for every finger. Try to obtain a dynamic consistency throughout the pattern, especially when using weaker fingers. Sliding from one position to the next could be challenging in terms of timing, make sure to not to lose track of the subdivisions!

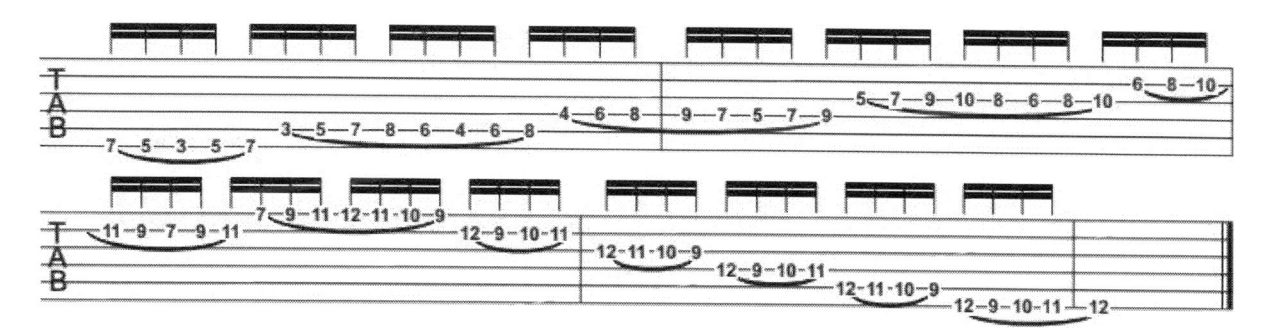

```
T|-----------------------------------------------------------5--7--9--10--8--6--8--10----------6--8--10-|
A|-----------------------3--5--7--8--6--4--6--8----4--6--8--9--7--5--7--9-----------------------------|
B|--7--5--3--5--7-----------------------------------------------------------------------------------|

T|--11--9--7--9--11--7--9--11-12-11-10--9----------------------12-11-10--9-------------------------|
A|------------------------------------12--9-10-11--12-11-10--9--------------12--9-10-11----------|
B|-------------------------------------------------------12--9-10-11--------------------12-------|
```

Crystal Cave

Category: Fretting & Picking Hand
Level: Advanced
Techniques: Finger Stretch, Fingerstyle

Description: When talking about left hand strengthening the first thing that comes to mind is some blistering scalar run across three octaves, but static tensions plays a major role in finger strength development. Hold these chords and arpeggiate them, trying to be as accurate as possible when changing position. Spread voicings can prove to be an effective warm-up strategy and stamina developing tool, just make sure not to strain your tendons.

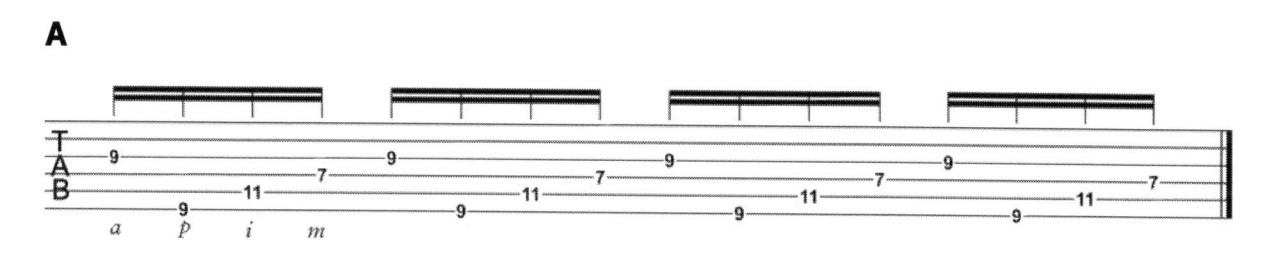

A

```
T|--9-----------------9-----------------9-----------------9-----------------|
A|--------7-----------------7-----------------7-----------------7----------|
B|----11--------------11--------------11--------------11-------------------|
     9                  9                  9                  9
     a  p  i  m
```

B

```
T ---8-----------------8-----------------8-----------------8---------------------
A -----11----------------11----------------11----------------11-------------------
B --------9-----------------9-----------------9-----------------9-----------------
  ---7-----------------7-----------------7-----------------7---------------------
```

C

```
T ---7-----------------7-----------------7-----------------7---------------------
A -----10----------------10----------------10----------------10------------------
B --------9-----------------9-----------------9-----------------9-----------------
  ---8-----------------8-----------------8-----------------8---------------------
```

D

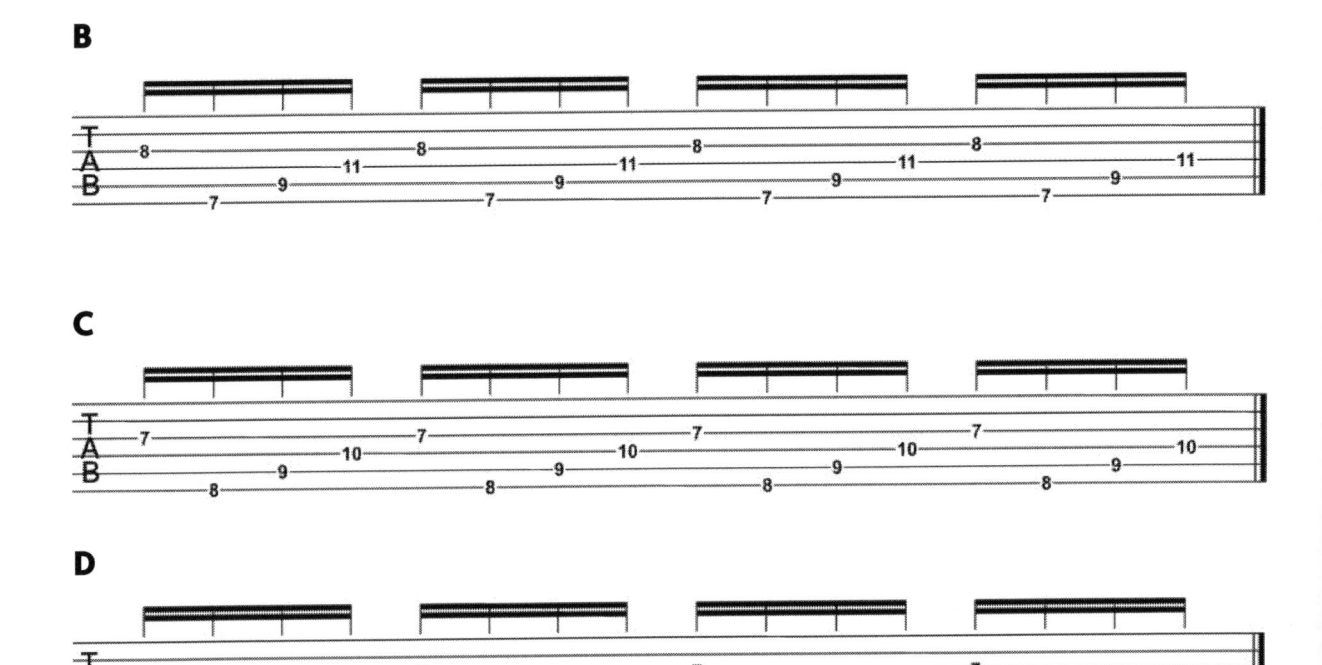

```
T ---7-----------------7-----------------7-----------------7---------------------
A -----5-----------------5-----------------5-----------------5-------------------
B --------8-----------------8-----------------8-----------------8-----------------
  ---6-----------------6-----------------6-----------------6---------------------
```

Spicy Neighbours

Category: Fretting & Picking Hand
Level: Advanced
Techniques: Alternate Picking, Economy Picking

Description: This lick constructed on the C Melodic Minor scale takes full advantage of chromaticisms to spice up its effect. Try different combinations of alternate and economy picking; a good strategy could be to alternate pick until the occurrence of the mini-sweep beginning on the "a" of the third beat, which would be economy picked, and then resume alternate picking.

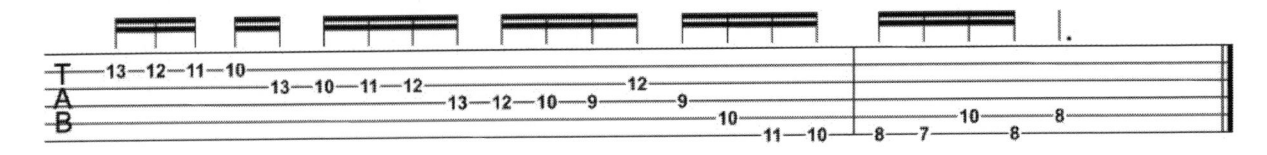

```
T --13-12-11-10-------------------------------------------------------------------
A --------------13-10-11-12-----------------12------------------------------------
B --------------------------13-12-10-9------9---10----------10----8---------------
                                        11-10--8-7------8-----------------------
```

Attack!

Category: Fretting & Picking Hand
Level: Advanced
Techniques: Alternate Picking

Description: This frantically aggressive modern rock riff targets your endurance through a series of wide movements in both the fretting and the picking hand. The 16th note triplets challenge both your timing and relaxation, and require complete familiarity with the phrase to be executed with confidence. Try palm muting the pitches played on the low E string which should add a percussive effect to the line.

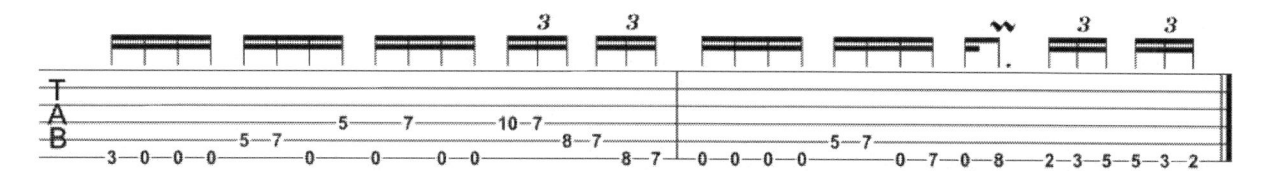

```
T|-------------------------------------------------|-----------------------------------------------|
A|-------------5---7-------------------10--7-------|-------------------------5---7-----------------|
B|--3--0--0----------5--7------0----0--------8--7--|--0--0--0--0-----0--7--0---8----2--3--5--5--3--2-|
                          0---- 0---- 0
```

Chapter #5

Play Faster and Accurately

My first love was the sound of guitar.
— Boz Scaggs

"I wish I could play faster!" I am sure every guitarist out there has had this thought at least once on their guitar journey. Well, that's absolutely fine, doesn't everything sound better when played faster?

Through this chapter, I intend on helping you play faster. We will be aiming to increase our overall speed and dexterity in this chapter. From beginner level techniques to advanced techniques, you will notice a significant increase in your speed levels once you are through with this chapter.

As the saying goes — to play faster, you have to first go slow. This is why I have provided a speed you can start with and the speed you should aim for in the tags for this chapter. Your objective should be to gradually increase your speed until you hit the desired target. Don't forget – the slower you practice, the faster you get.

So, get your metronome out! Let's begin!

Chromasweep

Category: Fretting & Picking Hand
Level: Beginner
Techniques: Sweep Picking

Starting BPM: 45
Goal BPM: 80

Description: This exercise focuses on the fundamental motion of sweep picking by trimming it down to its smallest terms. The chromatic nature of the line will allow you to easily internalise the fret pattern and therefore direct your active attention to the movement itself.

Be aware of the resonating unused strings, use your right palm to mute the low E and A strings while lightly touching the high E string with your fretting hand fingers.

The motion of the pick should be continuously flowing; make sure to find a comfortable angle at which to hold the pick and don't change it throughout the movement.

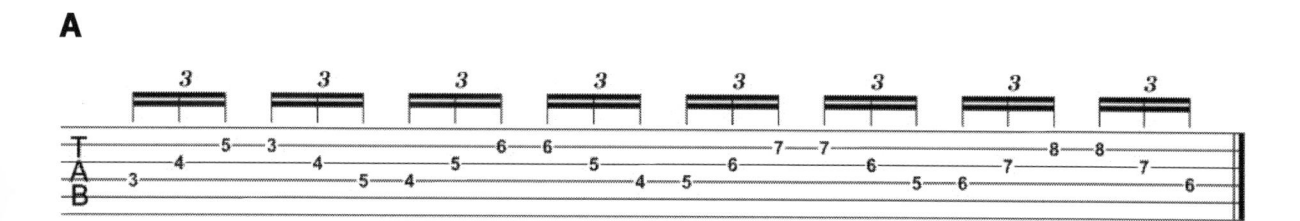

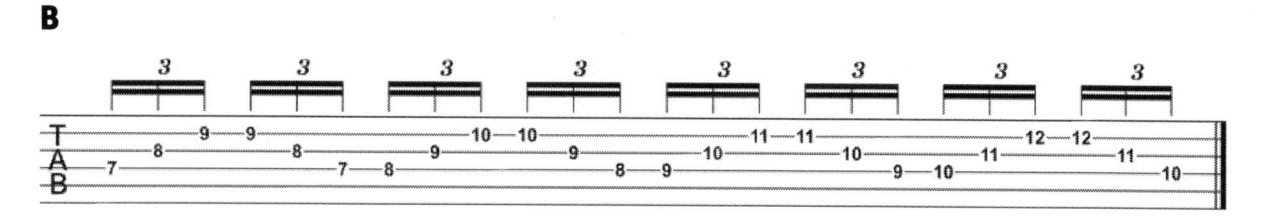

A

```
       3       3       3       3       3       3       3       3
T----5-3-----6-6-----7-7-----8-8-----
A--4---4-----5-5-----6---6-----7---7-
B-3-----5-4-----4-5-----5-6-----6---
```

B

```
       3       3       3       3       3       3       3       3
T-----9-9-----10-10-----11-11-----12-12-
A---8-----8-----9-----10-----10-----11-----11-
B-7-----7-8-----8-9-----9-10-----10-
```

The Ascent

Category: Fretting Hand
Level: Beginner
Techniques: Hammer-On

Starting BPM: 50
Goal BPM: 80

Description: The building block of hammer-on exercises: the single string scale over a pedal tonic. It's simple in its premise, but requires some dedication to master. Don't get carried away and aim at cohesion and precision of attack throughout the phrase.

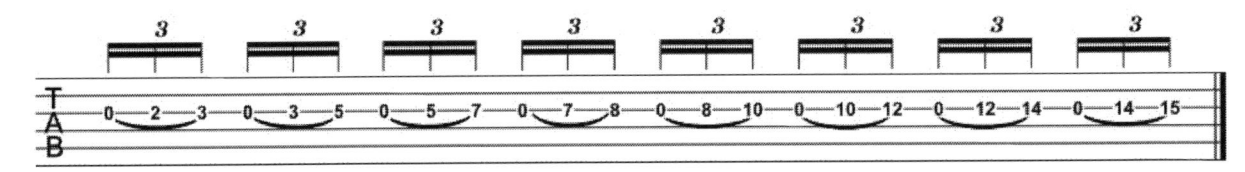

```
     3       3       3       3       3       3       3       3
T|--0--2--3--0--3--5--0--5--7--0--7--8--0--8--10--0--10--12--0--12--14--0--14--15--|
A|
B|
```

The Descent

Category: Fretting Hand
Level: Beginner
Techniques: Pull-Off

Starting BPM: 40
Goal BPM: 80

Description: Once you've reached the peak, you've got to come down.

Slightly more challenging than it's hammer-on variation, this exercise will develop accuracy and strength calibration in your fretting hand; vital elements for a seamless execution of the pull-off.

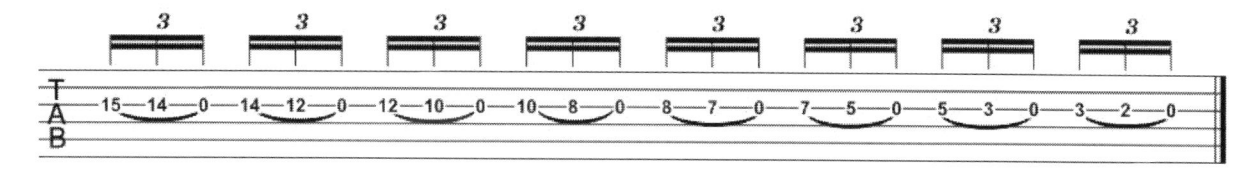

```
    3       3       3       3       3       3       3       3
T|-15-14-0-14-12-0-12-10-0-10-8-0-8-7-0-7-5-0-5-3-0-3-2-0-|
A|
B|
```

Fire in The Cabin

Category: Fretting Hand
Level: Beginner
Techniques: Hammer-On

Starting BPM: 100
Goal BPM: 150

Description: A brief ascending pentatonic pattern in the style of many rockers.

The hammer-on technique is well suited to blistering speeds, but dynamic consistency and articulation should always be your primary goal, so don't get tempted by cranking up the metronome straight-away, and listen to every nuance of the line!

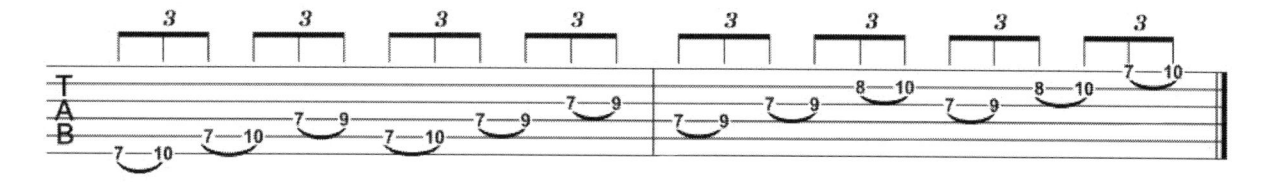

```
       3       3       3       3       3       3       3       3
T|                                           8-10    8-10  7-10
A|             7-9     7-9     7-9    7-9
B|-7-10  7-10        7-10
```

Fire in The Cockpit

Category: Fretting Hand
Level: Beginner
Techniques: Pull-Off

Starting BPM: 80
Goal BPM: 150

Description: The pull-off counterpart to the previous exercise. Much more challenging, as it requires greater finger strength and coordination to produce an accurate output.

Start slow and play your way up slowly but surely; this technique requires patience, practise it a little bit every day for better results.

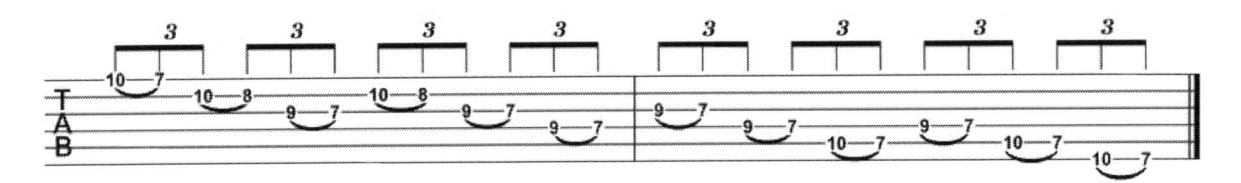

```
    3    3    3    3     3    3    3    3
T|-10-7------------------|----------------------|
A|------10-8---10-8---9-7|-9-7------------------|
B|--------9-7-----9-7----|-----10-7-9-7--10-7---|
                                        -10-7
```

Eerie Sweeps

Category: Fretting & Picking Hand
Level: Intermediate
Techniques: Sweep Picking, Economy Picking

Starting BPM: 60
Goal BPM: 110

Chapter #5. Play Faster and Accurately

Description: This series of phrases is based on the fourth and fifth modes of B Harmonic Minor and combines the incorporation of the 6th in the arpeggios along with short scalar passages. The resulting pattern calls for the combined employment of sweep and economy picking to be properly executed. Always keep economy of motion in mind, and work out which fingering is best adaptable to your personal technique.

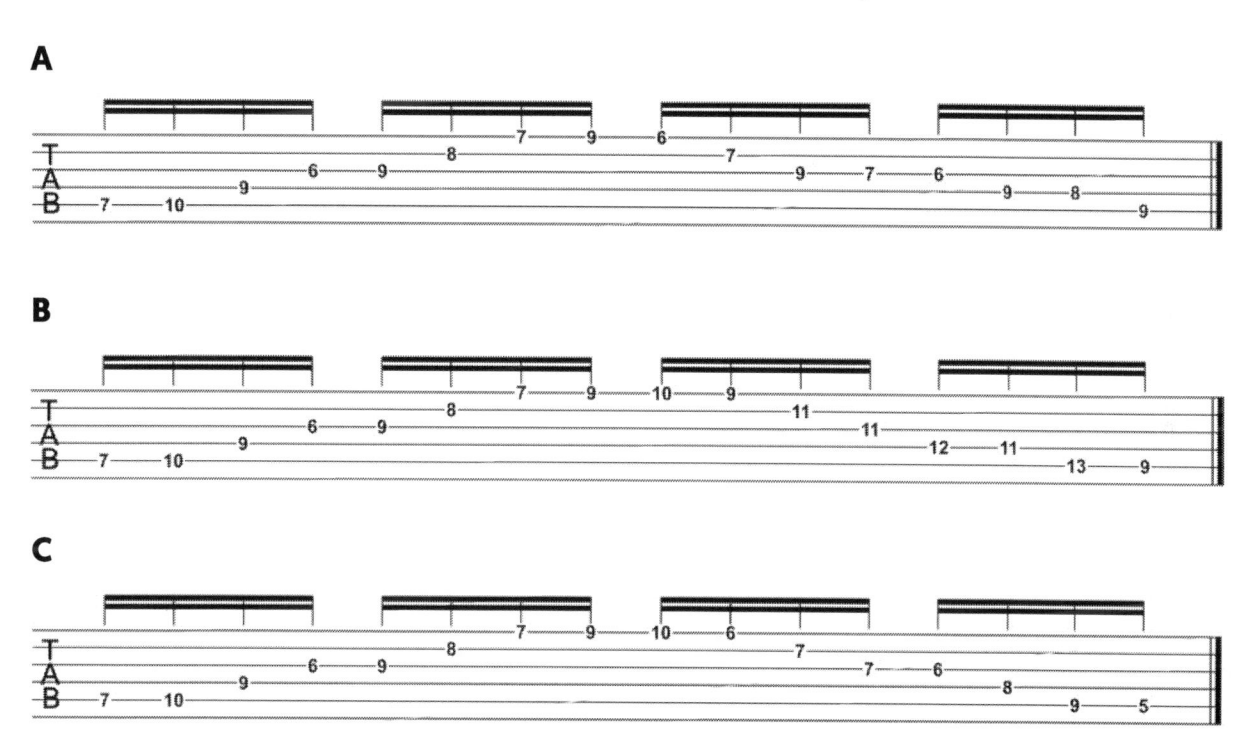

A

```
T|--------------------8--7--9--6--------7-------------------|
A|----------6--9-----------------------9--7--6--------------|
B|-7--10-9-------------------------------------9--8--9------|
```

B

```
T|--------------------8--7--9--10--9--11--------------------|
A|----------6--9----------------------11--12--11------------|
B|-7--10-9---------------------------------------13--9------|
```

C

```
T|-----------------7--9--10--6-------7----------------------|
A|----------6--9---------------8---------7--6---------------|
B|-7--10-9-------------------------------------8--9--5------|
```

Three by Five

Category: Fretting Hand
Level: Intermediate
Techniques: Finger Stretching

Starting BPM: 90
Goal BPM: 140

41

Description: A very unorthodox approach to pentatonic playing: rather than opting for a two-note-per-string pattern, the third note is played on the same string and then repeated on the adjacent one. The result is a great finger stretching routine, bearing an interesting musical effect to incorporate in your playing.

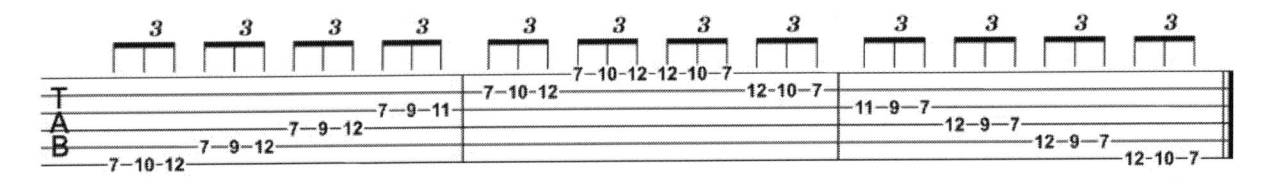

```
3   3   3   3    3   3   3   3     3   3   3   3
                       7-10-12-12-10-7
                 7-10-12            12-10-7
          7-9-11                              11-9-7
     7-9-12                                         12-9-7
7-10-12                                                   12-9-7
                                                               12-10-7
```

Just Tap Water for Me

Category: Fretting & Picking Hand
Level: Intermediate
Techniques: Tapping

Starting BPM: 80
Goal BPM: 130

Description: A well-executed tapping phrase will have sensational effects on a crowd but, while it might seem like a daunting technique at first, a little bit of consistent practice will go a long way. Get the basics down with these two phrases, the first one incorporating open strings and the second one being purely scalar.

For the tapped note you could either use your index or middle finger, experiment with both to find out which one comes more comfortable to you.

While the initial attack of the tap provides thrust to the pattern, the left-hand legato will maintain said thrust alive; ensure dynamic consistency and prevent adjacent strings from resonating.

A

```
T         T         T         T
T-12--8--5--0---12--8--5--0---13--0--5--8---15--0--5--8--
A
B
```

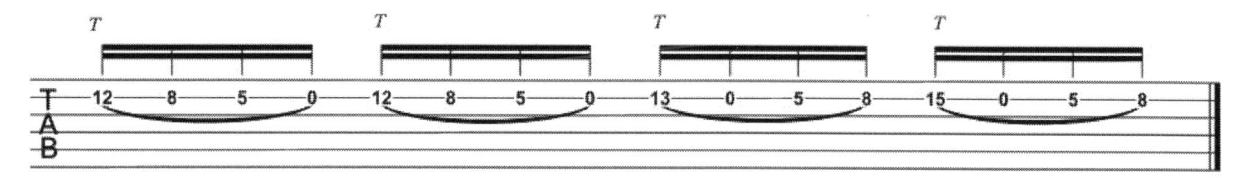

B

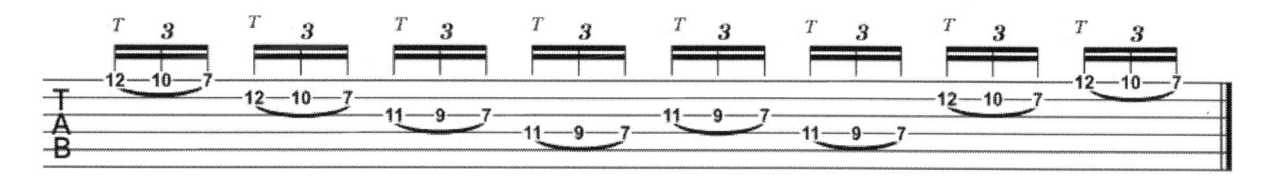

```
T 3   T 3   T 3   T 3   T 3   T 3   T 3   T 3
T-12-10-7-----------------------------------------12-10-7--12-10-7-
A--------12-10-7-----------------11-9-7--12-10-7-------------------
B----------------11-9-7--11-9-7-----------------------------------
```

Peckin' Around

Category: Fretting & Picking Hand
Level: Intermediate
Techniques: Legato, Chicken Picking

Starting BPM: 75
Goal BPM: 115

Description: This brief pentatonic riff presents a few chromaticisms to provide some exercise to all four fingers. Attack the D string with your pick while plucking the G string with your middle finger. The hardest challenge of this line is evenness of articulation, especially considering the presence of the finger-roll in the third beat of the pattern.

Don't be afraid to keep a lower tempo until you've mastered the basic motion behind the exercise.

```
T|--------5---------6---------7---------8-----|--------5---------6---------7---------8-----|
A|--5-7-----7-5-7-----7-5-7-----7-5-7-----7---|--5-7-----7-5-7-----7-5-7-----7-5-7-----7---|
B|--------------------------------------------|--------------------------------------------|
```

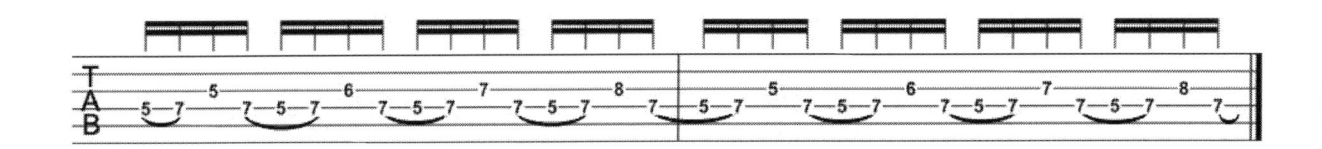

Ripples in The Water

Category: Fretting
Level: Intermediate
Techniques: Holdsworthian Legato, Economy Picking

Starting BPM: 60
Goal BPM: 110

Description: In this task we explore another kind of legato made famous by fusion player Allan Holdsworth. This technique avoids the use of pull-offs, making legato solely a tapping effort. Descending motions can prove particularly difficult, as they require lifting off the finger playing the higher pitch first and then tapping a lower note with another finger, relying on seamless coordination. However, the technique has its advantages, such as ease of transition between legato and other techniques, and general consistency of articulation.

As always, start at a comfortable tempo and only increase the mark when you're in full control of every note played.

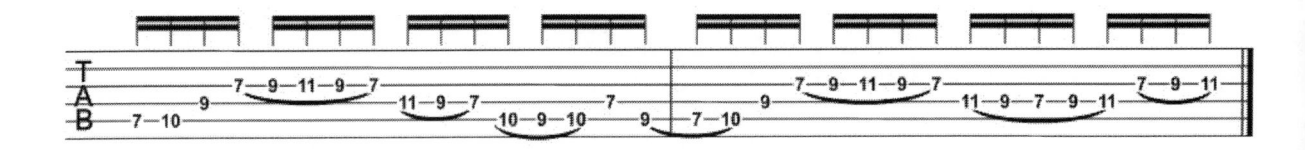

```
T|------7-9-11-9-7-----------------7-----|------------7-9-11-9-7-------------------7-9-11-|
A|----9-----------11-9-7---------9-------|--------9--------------11-9-7-9-11-------------|
B|-7-10----------------10-9-10-9---7-10--|----7-10---------------------------------------|
```

Seventh Seal

Category: Fretting & Picking Hand
Level: Intermediate
Techniques: Economy Picking

Starting BPM: 65
Goal BPM: 105

Description: Chained seventh arpeggios requiring position shifting and economy picking.

The addition of slide and legato passages eases the transition between positions, and adds some variation in texture.

Maintain a constant angle between the pick and the strings, relying predominantly on the wrist to carry out the motion, but slightly adjusting the forearm to accommodate the six string spread of the pattern.

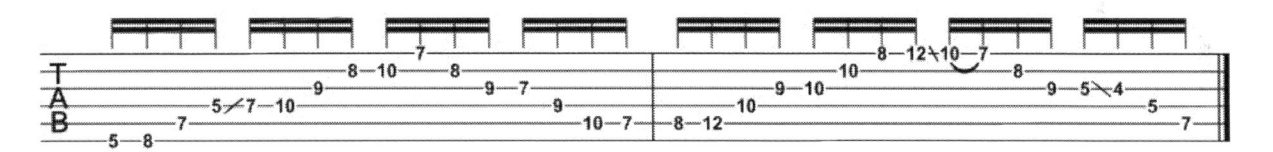

```
T|-------------------------7-------------------------------8-12-10-7----------|
A|------------------8-10--8----------------9-10--------10-----------8---------|
 |-------------5-7-10------------9-7--9------------9-10------------9-5-4------|
B|--------7---------------------10-7-------8-12---------------------------5---|
 |---5-8------------------------------------------------------------------7---|
```

Sliding Over Steps

Category: Fretting Hand
Level: Intermediate
Techniques: Slide

Starting BPM: 70
Goal BPM: 130

Description: A cascade of ascending and descending diatonic slides targeting accuracy and dexterity. Working out the best fingering for the pattern can be tricky, consider every option while trying to make it sound as graceful and continuous as possible.

Treat it as a monophonic synth line, there should be no overlap between pitches and minimal string noise should be produced.

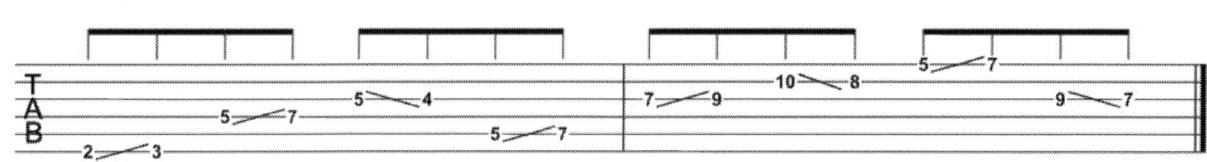

A

B

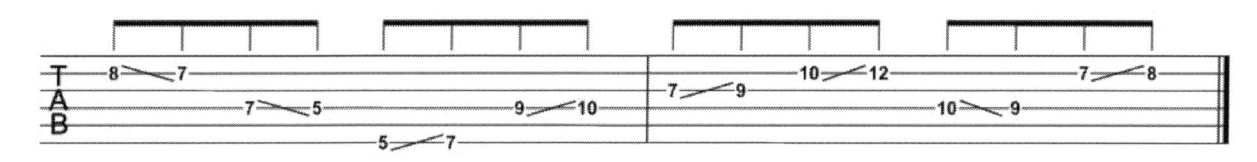

String Skip Legato

Category: Fretting Hand
Level: Advanced
Techniques: String Skipping, Legato

Starting BPM: 90
Goal BPM: 150

Description: An intricate scalar phrase, making full use of legato and string skipping.

Try parallel techniques such as chicken picking and Holdsworthian legato to give it a twist.

The biggest challenge of the pattern is reducing string noise down to a minimum while ensuring a consistent articulation of picked and slurred pitches.

Allow at least a week of practice at a moderate speed to internalise the movement, and increase the tempo gradually, without causing any strain to your tendons.

A

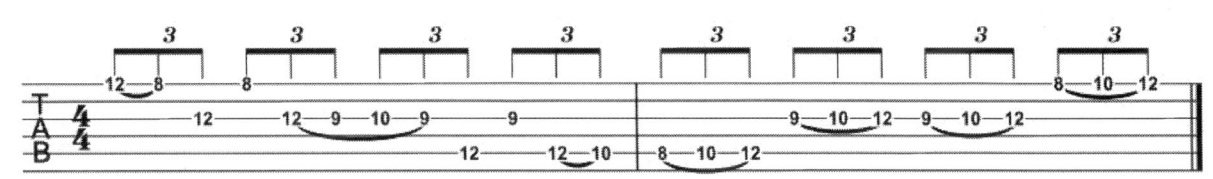

B

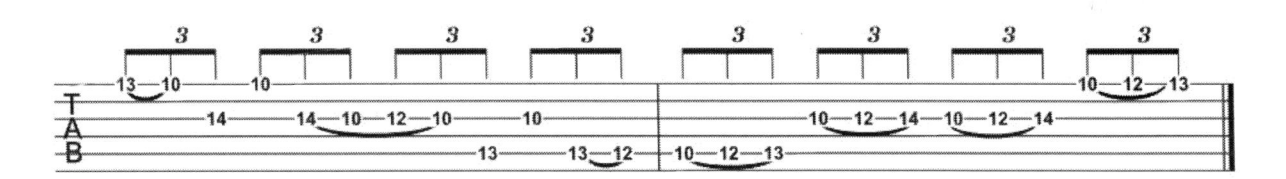

I'll Get a Lift

Category: Fretting & Picking Hand
Level: Advanced
Techniques: Legato, Chicken Picking, String Skipping

GUITAR EXERCISES

Starting BPM: 80
Goal BPM: 130

Description: These two phrases make unconventional use of scale boxes, incorporating string skipping to accommodate wider intervals, and using legato for ease of playability.

The initial attack of the notes is the most crucial element, assign your pick to the G string and your middle finger to the high E string, ensuring that the notes played on the latter are as intelligible as the ones played on the former.

A

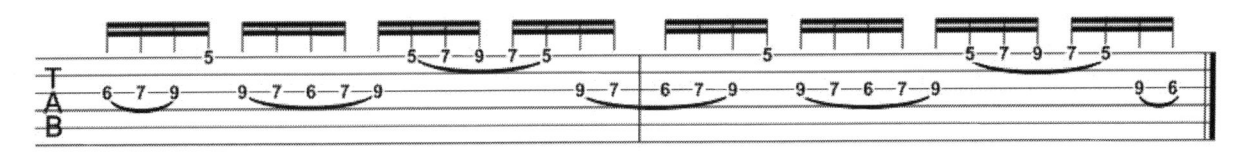

B

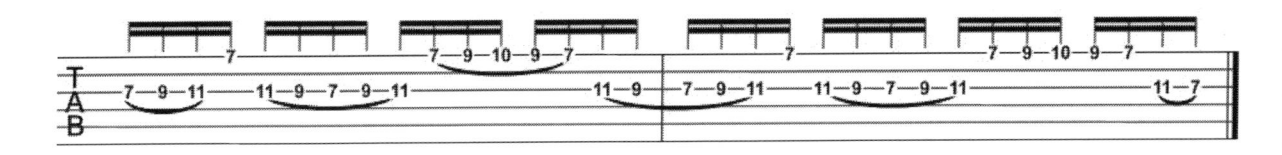

Trail Mix

Category: Fretting & Picking Hand
Level: Advanced
Techniques: Legato, String Skipping, Economy Picking, Slide

Starting BPM: 70
Goal BPM: 105

Description: This constant 16ths melodic phrase is a feat in coordination and accuracy.

It incorporates several techniques along with a position shift, requiring great care in articulation, dynamics, and economy of motion. Aim to produce a flowing and musical result without any stutter, decreasing the starting tempo if necessary.

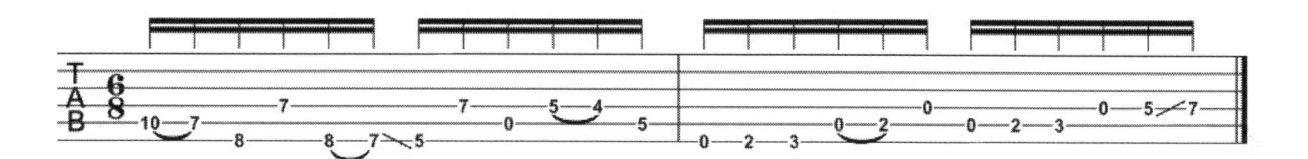

Chapter #6

Tame Your Picking Hand

The guitar chose me.
— Charlie Byrd

What do you do when you can't nail a solo or play a song the way it's meant to be played? You practice for hours, together, focusing on each and every fret you play. But what about your other hand? After all, you need two hands to be able to play well.

The Picking hand is probably the most ignored while learning guitar. It is expected to keep up with the fretting hand with no effort taken to concentrate and improve it. For all you know, you might be failing at playing what you want all because your picking hand is not good enough.

I am here to offer you a solution. A solution that will passively increase your guitar skills by targeting the most ignored part of your guitar journey.

Also, this chapter will not have a category section in the tags as all of them are aimed at the picking hand.

Starting The Engine

Level: Beginner
Techniques: Alternate Picking

Description: A series of exercises targeting the fundamentals of alternate picking, completely executed on open strings to allow you to focus solely on your picking hand.

Change of subdivision, odd groupings, even groupings, this task covers all the basics for having a productive start.

A

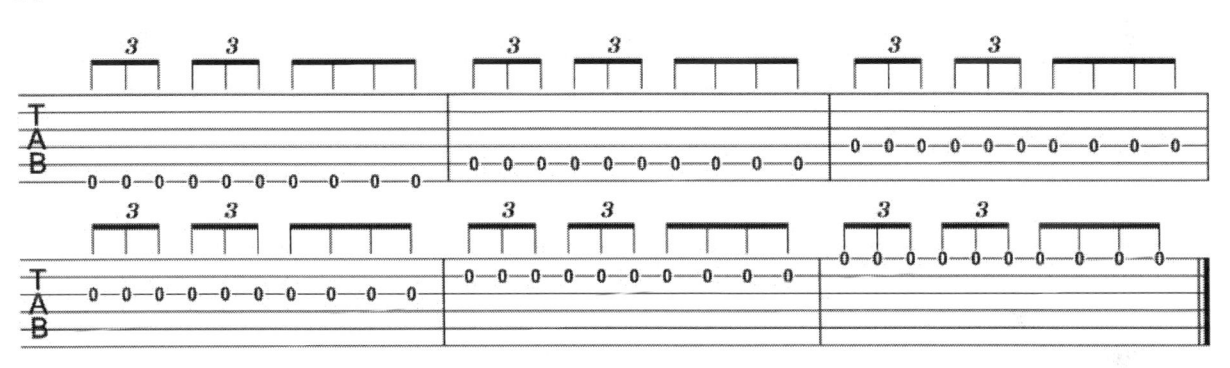

B

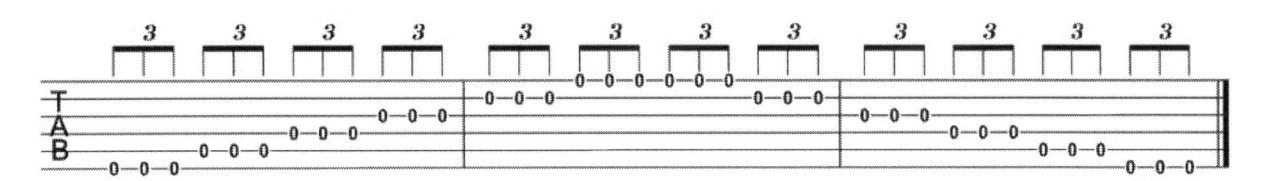

C

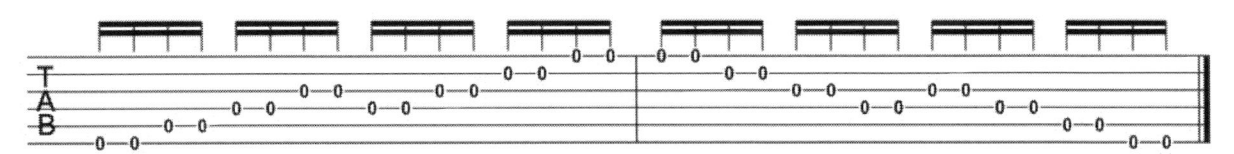

Pima Puma

Level: Beginner
Techniques: Fingerstyle

Description: Doesn't get much simpler than this. Put your pick on the side and let's get those fingers to work. Don't keep your wrist too close to the body of the guitar, as the motion should come from moving the metacarpal bones, and not by flexing the joints in a clenching fashion.

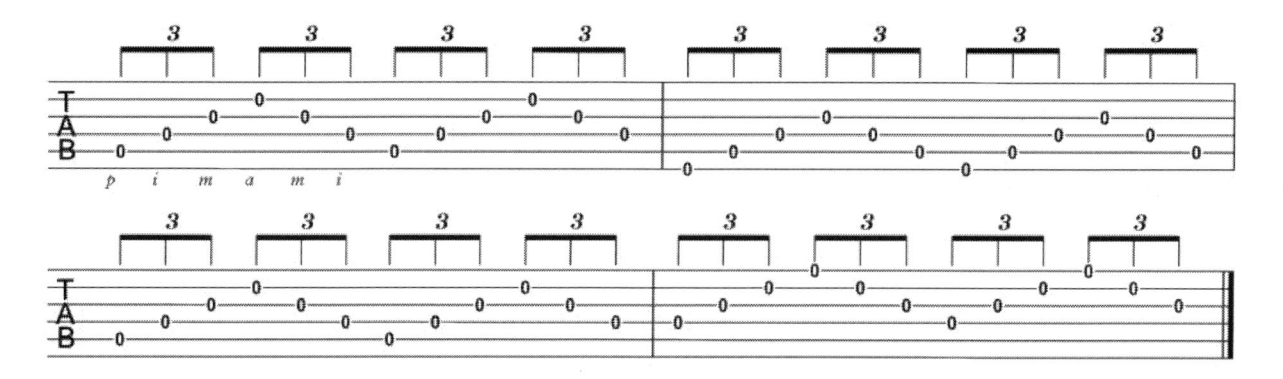

The Hen's Walk

Level: Beginner
Techniques: Chicken Picking

Description: This simple exercise targets coordination and facility with alternating between stroked notes and plucked ones. Always attack with a downstroke, and follow with a decise pop with your middle or ring fingers. The biggest challenge of this technique is to obtain a constant volume between both picked and plucked notes, try softening your pick attack as plucking too hard with your fingers might cause blisters to form.

```
T ---------------------|------------------0---------0-|--------0---------0-|-0---------0---------0-||
A -----0---------0-----|----0---------0---------0----|0---------0---------|---------0---------0---||
B -0---------0---------|0---------0------------------|--------------------|-----------------------||
   a   m   a   m
```

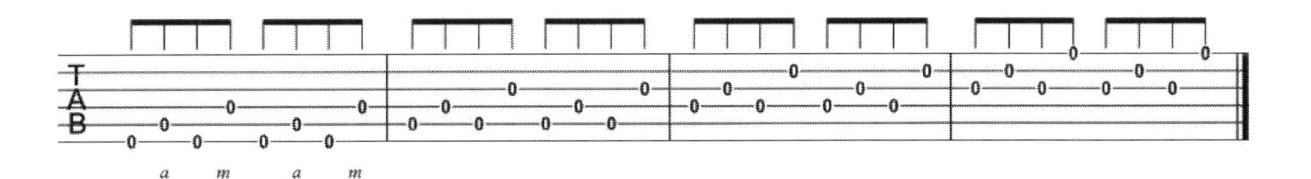

Three Feet Under

Level: Beginner
Techniques: Downpicking

Description: Downpicking can be a daunting technique, just a few minutes of intense practice can cause tension and discomfort in the wrist joint. Take it easy with some repeated pitch triplets, the fretting hand pattern is easy enough for you to concentrate on your picking hand relaxation. Maintain a consistent level of dynamics throughout, especially when changing strings.

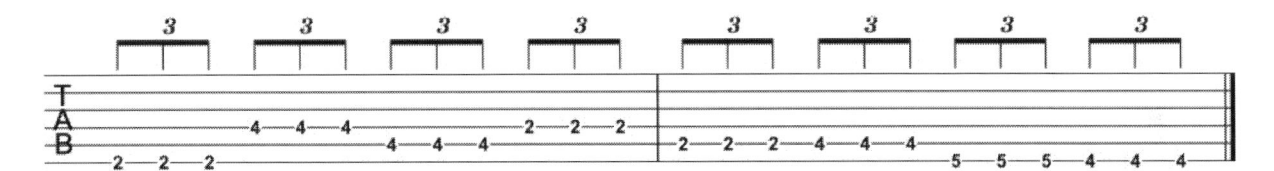

```
       3        3        3        3            3        3        3        3
T --------------------------------------------|-------------------------------------------||
A -------4—4—4----------2—2—2-----------------|-2—2—2---4—4—4-----------------------------||
B --------------4—4—4----------------- --------|----------------5—5—5---4—4—4--------------||
  2—2—2--------------------------------       |                                           ||
```

Bottom Up

Level: Intermediate
Techniques: Sweep Picking

Description: Try your sweep picking skills with a basic triadic progression on the top three strings. Only increase the tempo when the movement is in continuous flow, and all pitches are equally articulated. Sweep picking is one of those techniques that require patient practice for good results, spend a week or two just getting comfortable with the movement.

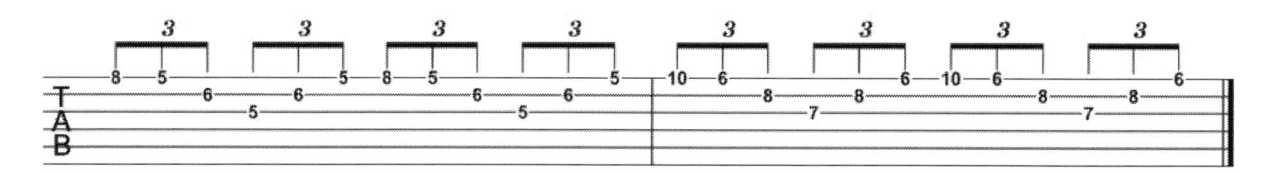

To The Sun and Back

Level: Intermediate
Techniques: Alternate Picking, String Skipping

Description: An ascending major scale where every pitch is alternated to the octave of the tonic. This requires a downstroke followed by an upstroke on another string, calling for a controlled and economic motion of the wrist. Experiment with pick angles, it really makes a difference.

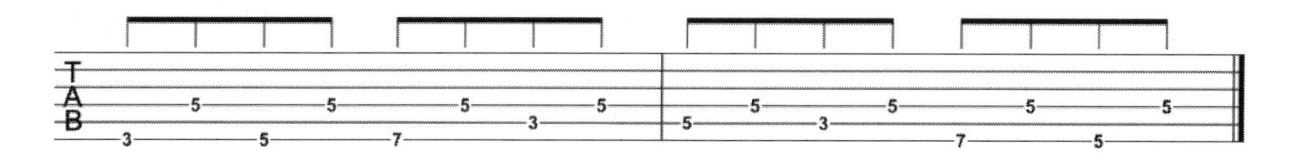

Jump The Rope

Level: Intermediate
Techniques: Alternate Picking, String Skipping

Description: A pentatonic lick with a twist, the wider intervals caused by string skip make for an interesting effect, but require particular coordination to maintain a flow and continuity throughout the pattern. Progressively move your forearm downwards as you get into the higher register.

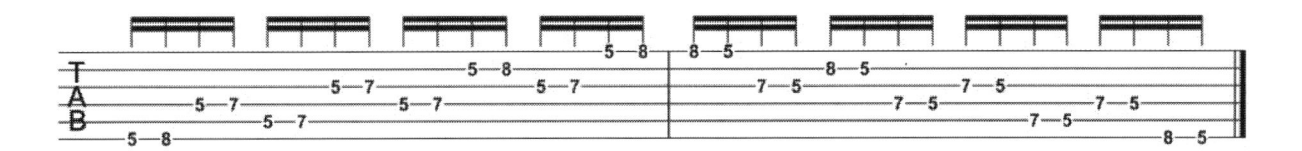

```
E|--------------------------------------------------|
B|--------------------------------------------------|
G|------------------5--8----8--5--------------------|
D|----------5--7------------------7--5--------------|
A|----5--7------------------------------7--5--------|
E|--5--8--------------------------------------8--5--|
```

Economy 101

Level: Intermediate
Techniques: Economy Picking

Description: A simple scalar phrase to test your economy picking. Always try and produce a single motion when playing two adjacent strings, the economy is lost if you break down the movement, you might go bankrupt!

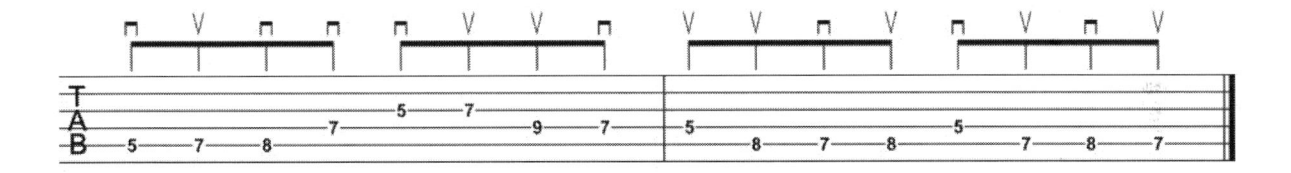

```
E|--------------------------------------------------|
B|--------------------------------------------------|
G|----------------5--7----------5---------5---------|
D|----------7----------9--7--------7--8------7--8--7|
A|--5--7--8------------------8----------------------|
E|--------------------------------------------------|
```

Middle Ground

Level: Intermediate
Techniques: Sweep Picking

Description: Now that you're at ease with the fundamentals of sweep picking, try and add another string to the sequence. You'll now experience the first instances of string noise, manage it with a combination of your picking hand's palm and you fretting hand's fingers.

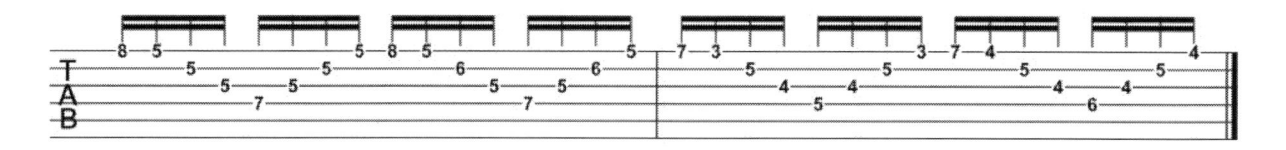

```
T|--8--5--------------5--8--5--------------------------------------3--7--4--------------------4-|
 |-----5--------5--------------------5--------5-----5-----------------------5-----------5-------|
A|--------5--5-----5-----------6--------5--5-----4-----4--------------------4-----4-------------|
 |-----------7--------------7-----------------------5----------------------------------6--------|
B|----------------------------------------------------------------------------------------------|
```

Soaring Waves

Level: Advanced
Techniques: Sweep Picking

Description: Same old progression, but now spanning a whopping five strings! String noise management is now paramount. You'll have to employ what is called "progressive palm muting", which is essentially lowering the side of your hand along the strings while you ascend. Try beginning the progression with an upstroke, it will allow you to ascend to the top with a single uninterrupted motion.

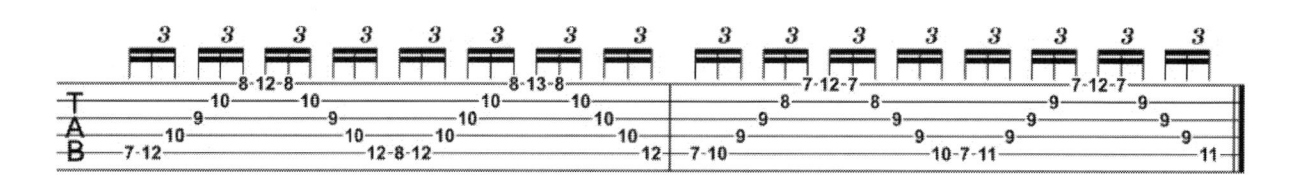

```
          3  3  3  3    3  3  3  3      3  3  3  3      3  3  3  3
T|------8-12-8---------------8-13-8----------------7-12-7---------------7-12-7-|
 |---10--------10---------10--------10----------8-------8-----------9-------9--|
A|-9-------9-------9---9--------9-------9----9-------9-------9---9-------9-----|
 |10-----------10---10----------10-----10---------------------9-------9--------|
B|7-12-------------------12-8-12-----------12--7-10--------10-7-11----------11-|
```

Chapter #7

Play Legendary Solos

The guitar was my weapon, my shield to hide behind.
— Brian May

Soloing! The best thing you can do on a guitar! You can noodle all day, replicate legendary solos, create your own style, the list is endless. In this chapter, we will tackle various scale patterns to help you nail that solo you have in mind!

We will tackle only scale exercises in this chapter. If you want to learn more about the technical aspects of scales and soloing, sign up for my newsfeed. I have a soon-to-be-released in-depth book on scales, which will teach you all you need to know about scales and mastering solos. You may download any of the bonuses on *www.theguitarhead.com/bonus* to be a part of the mailing list.

I might even give it away for free to those on my mailing list, so hurry! Sign up now!

Yin and Yang

Category: Picking & Fretting Hand
Level: Beginner
Techniques: Alternate Picking, Legato
Scale used: C Minor

Description: This exercise largely features the concept of opposites: an ascending triple followed by a descending one; a slurred triplet followed by fully picked one.

Learning single string scalar patterns enhances your understanding of the instrument, freeing horizontal rather than vertical movement.

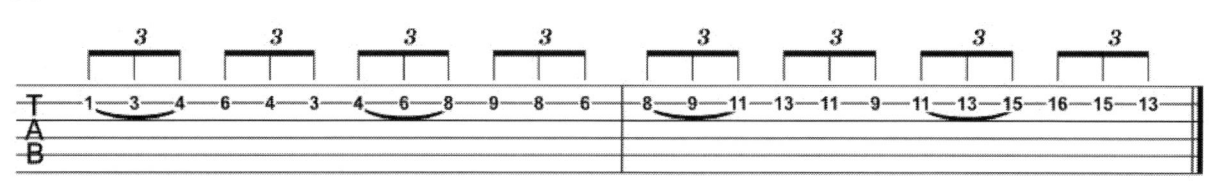

A

```
   3    3    3    3    3    3    3    3
E|-1-3-4-6-4-3-4-6-8-9-8-6-8-9-11-13-11-9-11-13-15-16-15-13-|
```

B

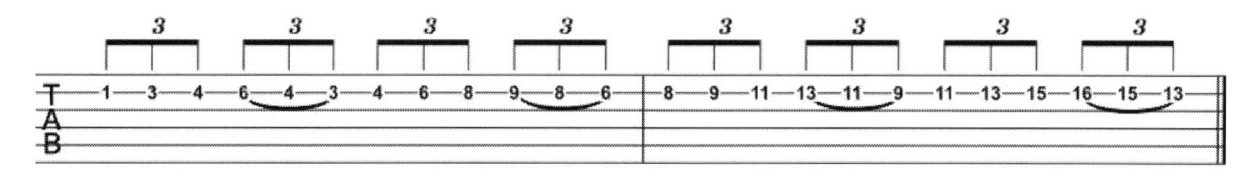

```
   3    3    3    3    3    3    3    3
E|-1-3-4-6-4-3-4-6-8-9-8-6-8-9-11-13-11-9-11-13-15-16-15-13-|
```

Just A Couple

Category: Fretting & Picking Hand
Level: Beginner
Techniques: Alternate Picking, Position Shifting
Scale used: A Minor Pentatonic

58

Description: A purely horizontal variation of the box shifts within the pentatonic scale.

In variation A, the four top notes of a box are played descending, before ascending to the next box, while in variation B the pattern is reversed. Try it with all couples of strings!

A

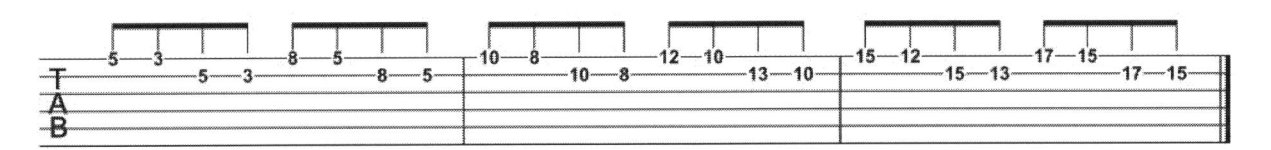

```
|----5--3-------8--5-------10--8-------12--10------15--12------17--15------|
|--------5--3------8--5--------10--8-------13--10------15--13------17--15--|
```

B

```
|--------15--17------12--15------10--12------8--10------5--8-------3--5----|
|----15--17------13--15------10--13------8--10------5--8-------3--5--------|
```

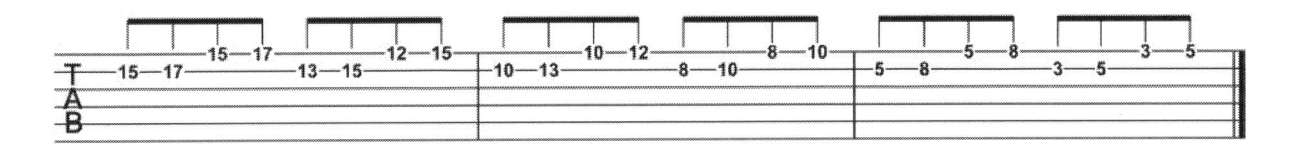

Rainy Morning

Category: Fretting & Picking Hand
Level: Beginner
Techniques: Alternate Picking, Finger Rolling
Scale used: E Dorian

Description: A simple melodic line based on the Dorian mode, it features the use of the finger roll in the Em11 arpeggio, as well as purely scalar passages, suggesting a further exploration of mixes of this kind to the player.

```
T
A    ———————————7———————————————————————————————————————7——————————10—8——7———————————————
B    —7—10———————9———7———————10———7———9—10—9—7—9—10—————7—10————————————————9———9—7—6————9—7———
                                                                                          10—9
```

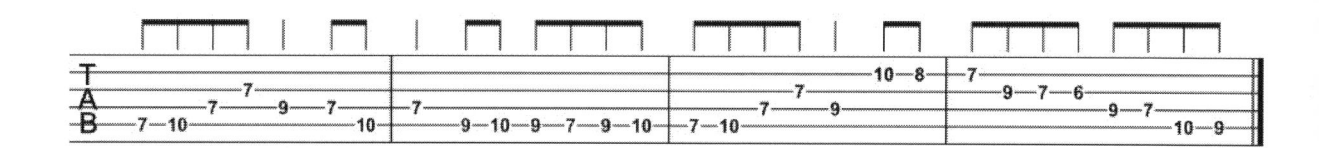

Sprints

Category: Fretting & Picking Hand
Level: Beginner
Techniques: Alternate Picking
Scale used: D Major

Description: A simple ascending and descending D major scale, alternating every two beats between 8th and 16th subdivisions. These speed bursts not only target your tempo feel, but also help you improve your ability to manage the tendency to increase tension in the wrist when accelerating.

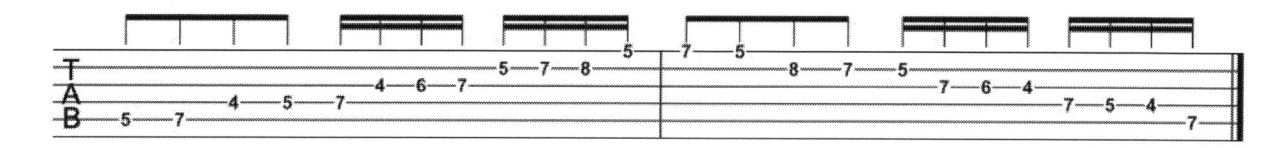

```
T                                    5—7—8       7—5      8—7—5
A              4—5—7        4—6—7                                 7—6—4
B    5—7                                                                   7—5—4
                                                                                 7
```

Car Chase

Category: Fretting Hand
Level: Intermediate
Techniques: Hammer-On
Scale used: D Major

Description: A blistering ascending scale pattern. It's easy forgo precision in hammer-ons only phrases, don't neglect your time, tone, and articulation when practising this exercise.

Chapter #7. Play Legendary Solos

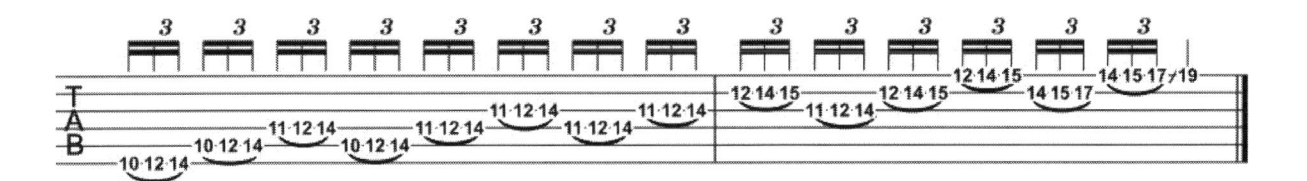

Just Perfect

Category: Fretting & Picking Hand
Level: Intermediate
Techniques: Alternate Picking, Finger Stretching
Scale used: G Major

Description: A simple succession of ascending perfect fifths spanning three octaves.

Two-note-per-string patterns do wonder for stamina and relaxation, and this exercise comes with the added benefit of a good stretching workout. Visualising and naming the notes on the neck will help you to break out of scale boxes, and in finding your way when soloing.

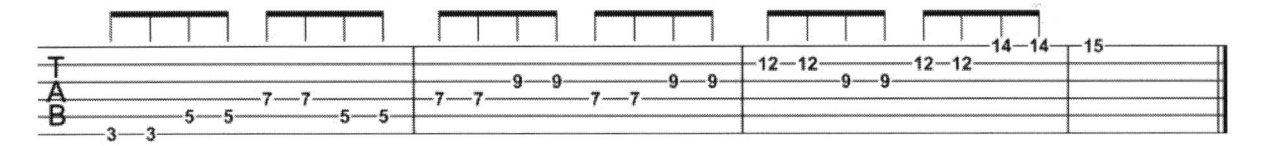

Cow Lick

Category: Picking Hand
Level: Intermediate
Techniques: Alternate Picking
Scale used: G Mixolydian

Description: This blues flavoured lick reminds you that open strings can be a strong ally even when your fretting hand is way up the neck! Always know the alterations of the key in which you're playing, this will tell you which open strings are diatonic to your tonality.

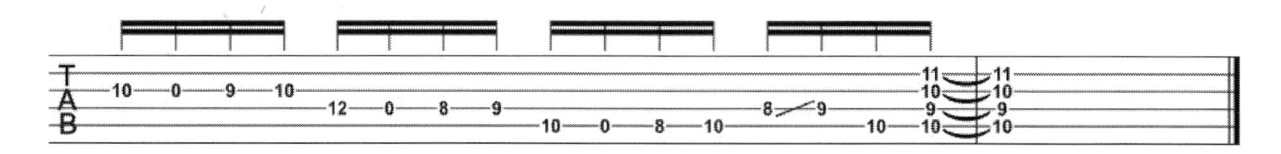

```
T|--10--0--9--10-----------------------------------------------11~-11--|
A|-------------12--0--8--9----------------8--9-----------10~-10--|
B|---------------------10--0--8--10---------10--10~-10--|
                                                        9~-9
```

Enclosing Beasts

Category: Picking Hand
Level: Intermediate
Techniques: Alternate Picking
Scale used: B Minor

Description: However, not every note you play when soloing must be diatonic to the key, in this exercise we explore the technique called "enclosure", which is approaching your target note both from above and below. In this instance we are starting a diatonic step above the note, then briefly playing the target note before descending another semitone, then finally resolving again to the wanted pitch.

```
T|--9--7--6--7-----------------------------------------------|
A|----------8--7--6--7--------8--7--6--7--7--6--5--6--------|
B|----------------9--7--6--7----------------------9--8--7--8--9|
```

Passing By

Category: Fretting & Picking Hand
Level: Intermediate
Techniques: Economy Picking, Legato, Slide
Scale used: A Mixolydian

Description: The following phrase incorporates several techniques, and forces the player outside of the initial box, by using two adjacent major triads to shift position.

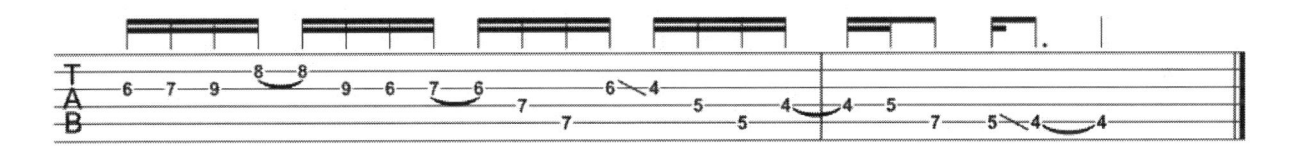

Move Those Boxes

Category: Fretting & Picking Hand
Level: Intermediate
Techniques: Alternate Picking
Scale used: A Minor Pentatonic

Description: A further exploration of horizontal shifts between the pentatonic boxes.

Beginning the new pattern on one of the pitches belonging to the previous box grants a certain continuity of sound, while allowing a greater reach up the instrument's neck.

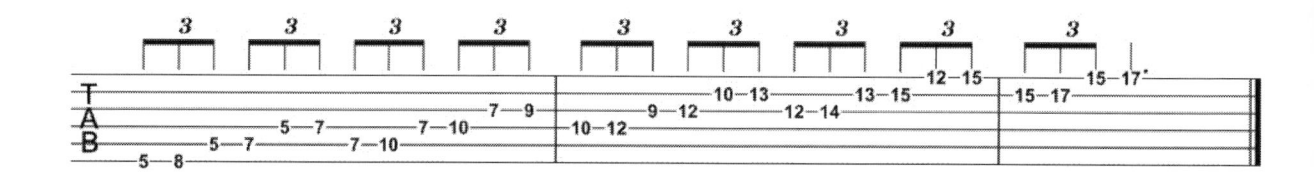

```
           3      3      3      3         3       3       3        3         3
T|---------------------------------------------------------------12-15-----15-17-|
A|------------------------------7-9---------------10-13------13-15---15-17--------|
B|-------5-7------7-10-------------------9-12--12-14------------------------------|
 |--5-8------------------------------10-12----------------------------------------|
```

Internal Triads

Category: Fretting & Picking Hand
Level: Intermediate
Techniques: Alternate Picking, Economy Picking,
Finger Stretching, Finger Roll
Scale used: G Major

Description: Triadic playing doesn't have to be purely chordal, individuating triads inside scale boxes will increase melodic control when soloing, and help outlining harmonic progressions. In variation A we see a sequence of ascending triads ascending up the scale, while in variation B a series of descending triads descending down the scale is played.

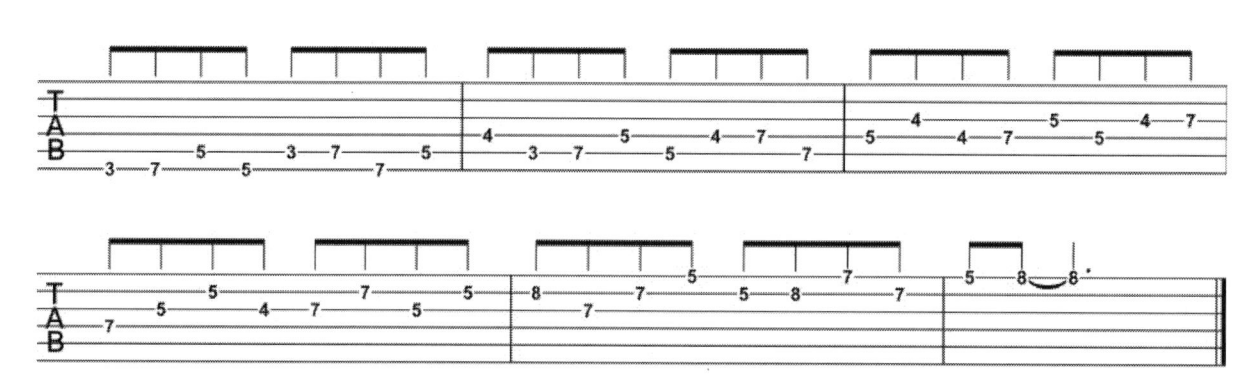

A

```
T|--------------------------------------------------------4------5------4-7-|
A|------5------3-7------5------4------5------4-7------5------4-7------5-----|
B|--3-7------5------7--------3-7------7--------------7----------------------|
```

```
T|----------------------------------------5------7------5--8~-8.|
A|------5------7------5--8------7------5------8------7-----------|
B|--7------4-7------5------7------7------------------------------|
```

Chapter #7. Play Legendary Solos

B

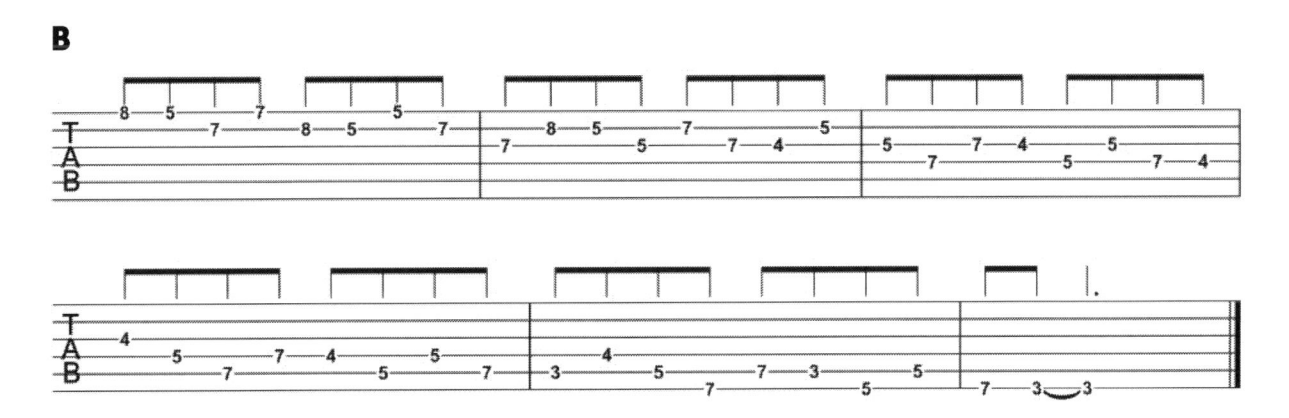

```
T|--8--5--7-----5-------|-----8--5--7-----5--|--5-----7--4-----5----|
A|--------7--8-----5--7-|--7--------5--7--4--|-----7--------5--7--4-|
B|----------------------|--------------------|----------------------|
```

```
T|--------4-----5-------|-----4-----5--7--3-----|--5--------7--3--3--|
A|-----5-----7-----4--5-|--5-----7--------5--5--|-----5--7-----------|
B|--7--------------5--7-|--3-----------------7--|--------------------|
```

Three Trees

Category: Fretting & Picking Hand
Level: Intermediate
Techniques: Alternate Picking
Scale used: E Minor

Description: The following exercise aims to suggest a different way of visualising the scale.

Intervallic playing, rather than a purely sequentially diatonic style, can provide some "space" in one's solos. This pattern specifically explores the interval of a diatonic third, but feel free to experiment with other intervals!

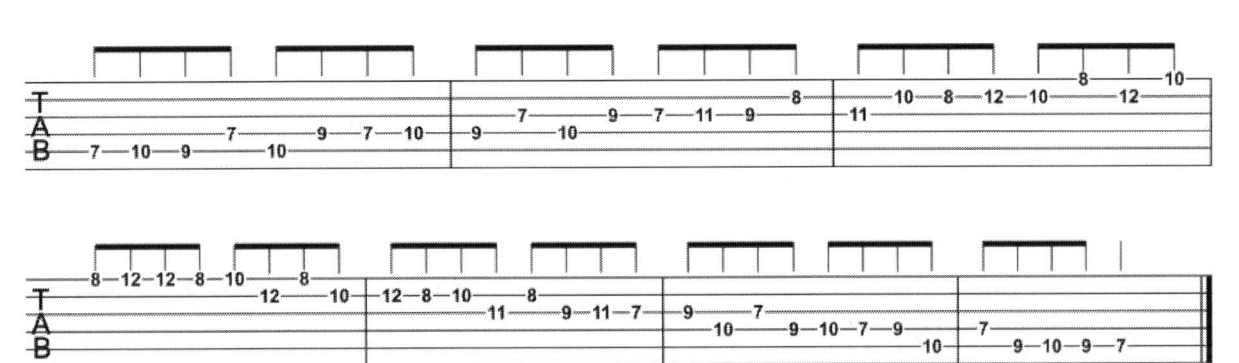

A

```
T|----------------------|-----------7-----8--|-10--8--12--10-----8--10-|
A|--------7-----9--7-10-|--9-----10---9-11-9-|-11----------12----------|
B|--7-10--9-10----------|-----------------   |                         |
```

```
T|--8-12-12-8-10--8----------------|--------7----------7---------|
A|-----------12-10-12-8-10----8----|--9--------9-10-7-9----------|
B|-----------------------11-9-11-7-|--------10------------9-10-9-7|
```

65

GUITAR EXERCISES

B

[guitar tablature]

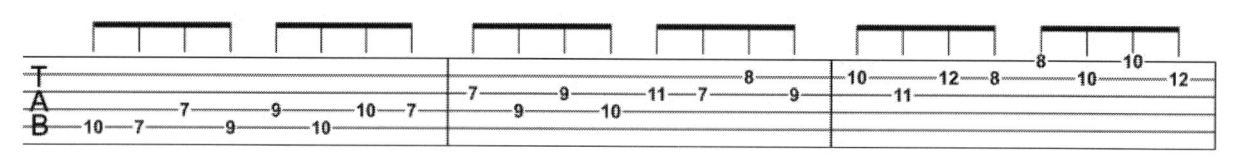

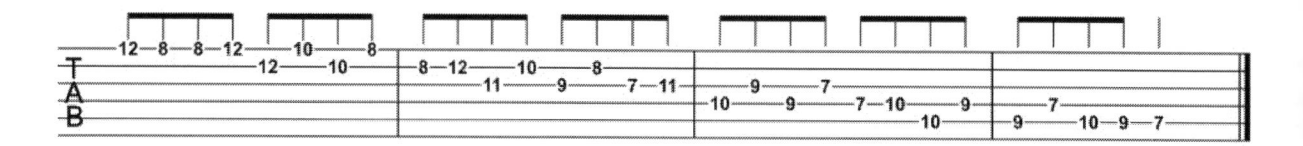

The Leap

Category: Fretting & Picking Hand
Level: Advanced
Techniques: Alternate Picking, String Skipping
Scales used:
A: F Dorian
B: G Phrygian
C: Ab Lydian

Description: An effective way to instantly freshen up your playing is simply changing your perspective on what you already know. This exercise is based on simple three-note-per-string scalar patterns, but omits every other string, resulting in an interesting mix of diatonic steps and leaps. Keep a loose wrist in your picking hand, always monitoring string noise, and minimise motion in the fretting hand.

A

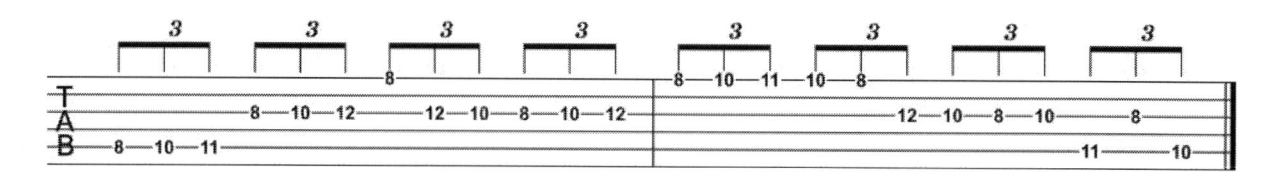

[guitar tablature]

B

```
        3           3           3           3              3           3           3           3
                              10                        10—11—13—11—10
            10—12—13      13—12—10—12—13                          13—12—10—12         10
   10—11—13                                                                      13      11
```

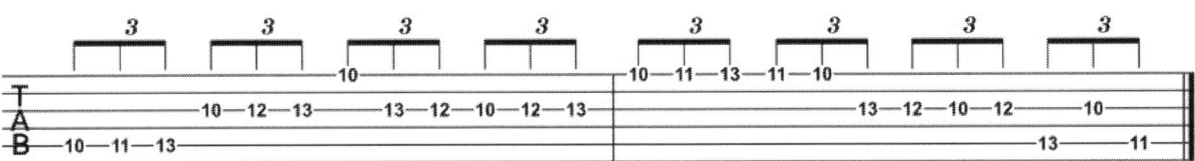

C

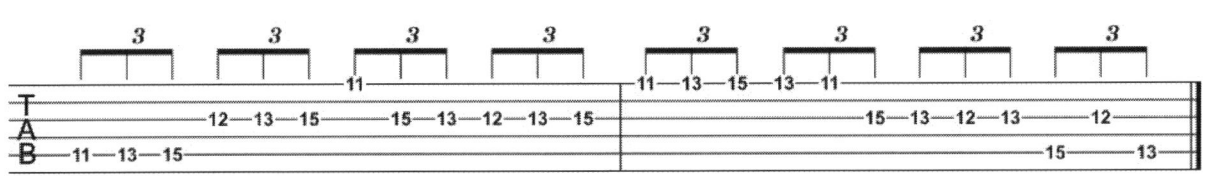

```
        3           3           3           3              3           3           3           3
                              11                        11—13—15—13—11
            12—13—15      15—13—12—13—15                          15—13—12—13         12
   11—13—15                                                                      15      13
```

That Escalated Quickly

Category: Fretting & Picking Hand
Level: Advanced
Techniques: Economy Picking, Finger Stretching
Scale used: A Minor Pentatonic

Description: When soloing using pentatonics it's common to gravitate around sequential patterns or licks we know, but arpeggios and uneven groupings of notes can be an effective tool to spice up your pentatonic playing. In this exercise we use a 2-1-3 notes per string pattern to outline an Am7 and a C6 arpeggios, and then repeating them up the octave.

The employment of economy picking adds an element of fluidity, unusual for a pentatonic line.

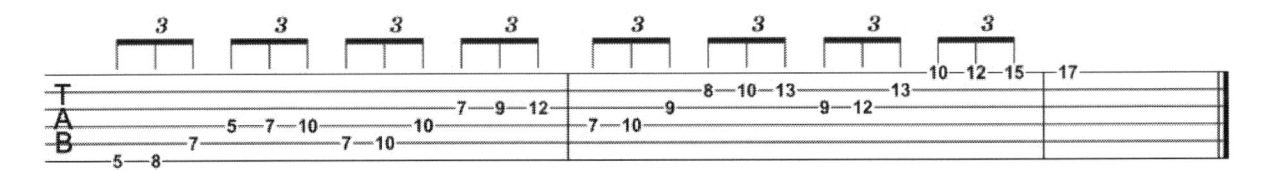

```
        3       3       3       3           3       3       3       3
                                                                      10—12—15  17
                                              8—10—13       13
                        7—9—12             9         9—12
            5—7—10  10                7—10
        7           7—10
   5—8
```

67

Climbing Back Up

Category: Fretting Hand
Level: Advanced
Techniques: Pull-Off
Scale used: B Minor

Description: The follow-up to "Car Chase", it features a pull-offs based descending pattern.

The repeated groups of three on every string make the challenge more manageable, although dynamic consistency and clear articulations will only come with time.

Make sure to practice this exercise only when fully warmed up.

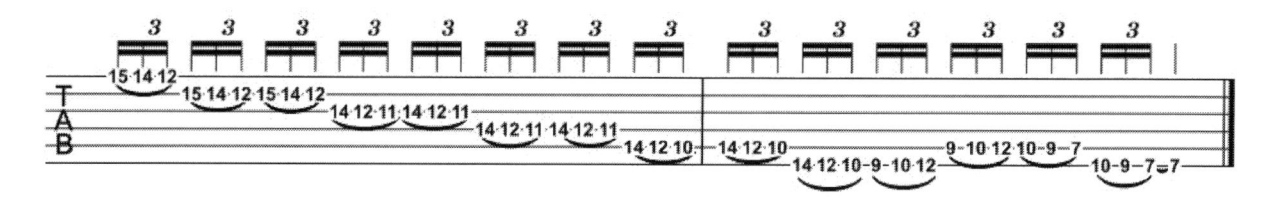

```
    3   3   3   3   3   3   3   3    3   3   3   3   3   3
  15-14-12
          15-14-12 15-14-12
                           14-12-11 14-12-11
                                            14-12-11 14-12-11
                                                             14-12-10  14-12-10                      9-10-12-10-9-7
                                                                              14-12-10-9-10-12                      10-9-7-7
```

Chapter #8

Master Chords & Arpeggio

All I have is this guitar, these chords and the truth.
— Jon Bon Jovi

Beginner chords to chords with names longer than the song itself. Chords are everywhere! Mastering them is essential, irrespective of your level of skill.

Through this chapter, we will master chords and Arpeggios through a series of exercises designed specifically for the fretting hand. Let's dive in!

Through Stained Glass

Level: Beginner
Techniques: Economy Picking

Description: One wouldn't necessarily think of arpeggiated open chords as an economy picking exercise, but applying such technique in this context makes for an effortless and more fluid comping. Keep your wrist loose and distant from the strings, to shortening their natural sustain through muting.

GUITAR EXERCISES

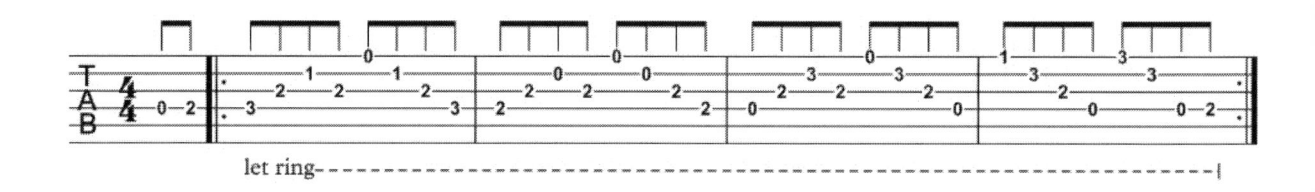

let ring- -

Raising The Barre

Level: Beginner
Techniques: Alternate Picking, Barre Chords

Description: Barre chords, as simple as they are, prove to be a valuable tool in the arsenal of every guitarist, and are incredibly useful as strengthening devices for the fretting hand as they engage all muscles in the hand and require consistency of grip for all strings to properly resonate.

Catch two birds with one stone by incorporating repeated 16th notes in the picking hand to develop relaxation and stamina in alternate picking.

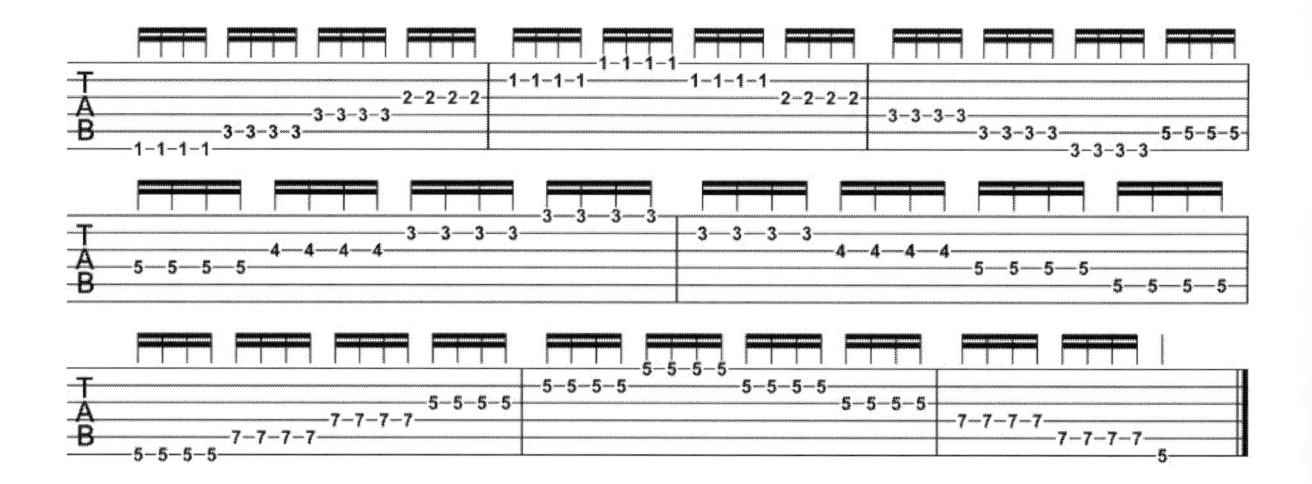

70

Chilling at Nine

Level: Intermediate
Techniques: Fingerstyle

Description: This exercise introduces the concept of independent bass movement through a simple ii-I" progression suitable to a modal landscape. Pluck the upper structure of the voicings with your index, middle, and ring fingers, while executing the simple bassline on the bottom two strings with your thumb. Once you're comfortable with this basic tonic to dominant movement, you can introduce increasingly complex and independent accompaniments in the thumb.

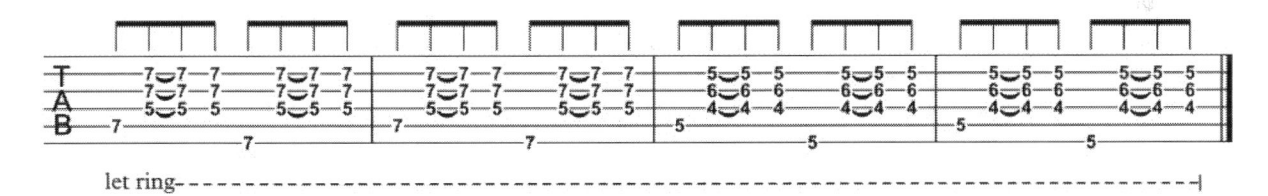

```
T-|--7~7-7----7~7-7----7~7-7----7~7-7----5~5-5----5~5-5----5~5-5----5~5-5--|
A-|--7~7-7----7~7-7----7~7-7----7~7-7----6~6-6----6~6-6----6~6-6----6~6-6--|
 -|--5~5-5----5~5-5----5~5-5----5~5-5----4~4-4----4~4-4----4~4-4----4~4-4--|
B-|--7--------------7----------7------------5------------5------------5----|
            -7-                                      -5-           -5-
```
let ring- -|

Fresh Moves

Level: Intermediate
Techniques: Strumming, Ghost-Notes

Description: A driving funk rhythm part, featuring abundant syncopation and ghost notes.

Always outline every 16th subdivision with your picking hand, hovering over the strings when not playing; this constant motion will help you keep track of not only the metronomic time, but also what's referred to as "pocket", or how well your part rhythmically interlocks with the whole ensemble.

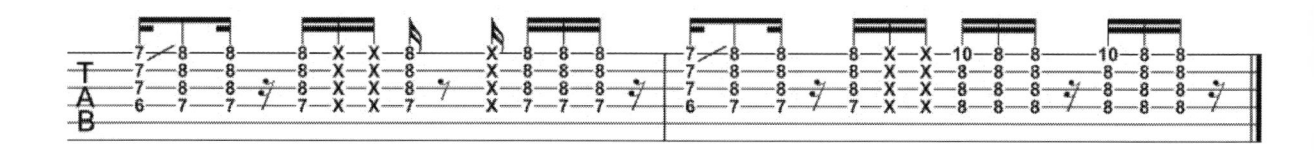

Suspension Bridge

Level: Intermediate
Techniques: Strumming

Description: A galloping succession of sus4 chords resolving to a major triad, these are a common harmonic device, especially useful when delaying resolution or building anticipation. The rhythmic subdivision, while simple, provides the player with a challenge in consistency. Always keep articulation and dynamics at the forefront of your practice.

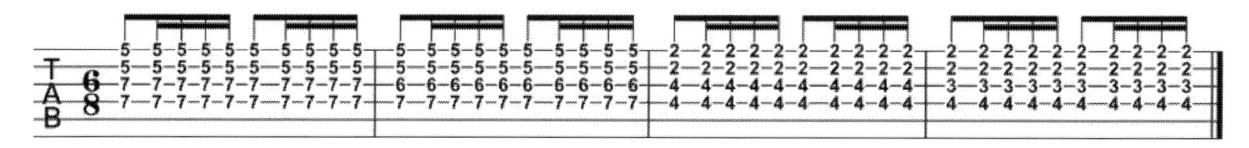

Sleepy Time

Level: Intermediate
Techniques: Fingerstyle

Description: A melodic bass part over a low-key arpeggiated triadic progression. The simultaneous plucking of two strings might require some adjustment in terms of coordination, begin by just combining a thumb stroke with index, middle, and ring fingers plucking if needed.

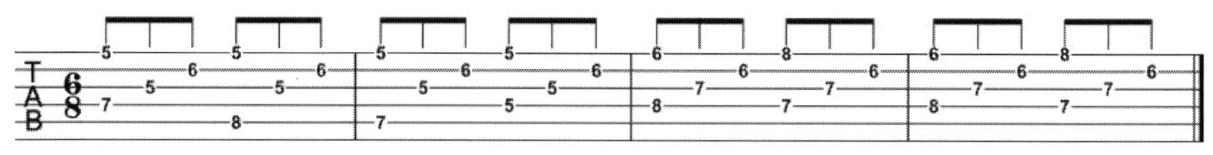

let ring-

Asking Questions

Level: Intermediate
Techniques: Fingerstyle

Description: Open strings can serve to generate interesting intervals when combined with fingered pitches up the neck. Use this ethereal sounding progression to develop your finger coordination when arpeggiating. If you want to focus solely on the plucking hand, pick an interesting static voicing and arpeggiate it with all different finger permutations in your plucking hand.

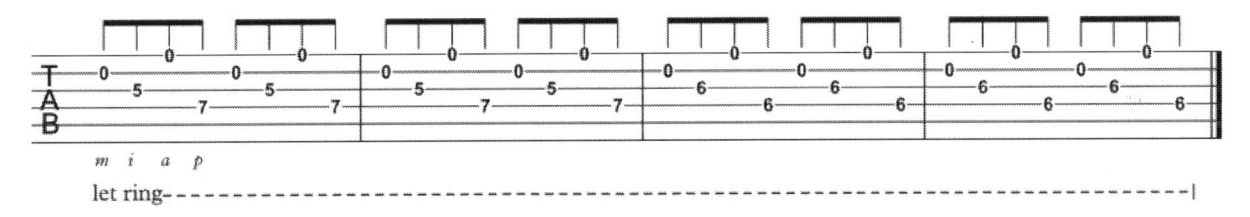

```
T|--0-----0-----0-----0-----0-----0-----0-----0-----0-----0-----0-----0--
A|----5-----5-----5-----5-----6-----6-----6-----6-----6-----6--
B|------7-----7-----7-----7-----6-----6-----6-----6-----6-----6-----6-----6--
  m  i  a  p
  let ring----------------------------------------------------------------|
```

A Drop in The Bucket

Level: Advanced
Techniques: Fingerstyle

Description: This finger-twisting chord progression challenges your endurance and ability to seamlessly transition between intricate voicings. It's constructed upon various inversions of Drop 2+4 voicings on the top four strings; these type of chords are a great way to spice up your comping, arpeggios, and even soloing, inserting intervals you wouldn't find in close position voicings.

```
T|--7-------7-------5-------7----
 |--5-------5-------5-------7----
A|--8-------6-------6-------8----
B|--6-------6-------4-------7----
```

Wait, I'm Confused

Level: Advanced
Techniques: Fingerstyle

Description: This melodic line features the occasional use of two distinct voices, and requires some dexterity to be properly executed. It encompasses several fingerstyle techniques, providing a well-rounded workout to insert in your routine.

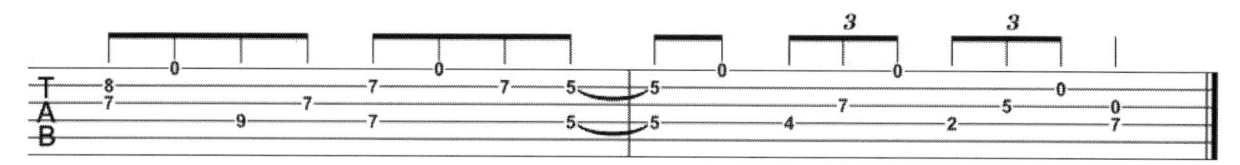

Ghostly Rhythms

Level: Advanced
Techniques: Strumming

Description: Speed bursts are a great way to improve relaxation in your wrist, and can also serve a musical purpose when playing in a funk rhythm setting. The infamous ghosted 32nds can breathe life into the most static of lines, but they are quite tricky to accurately execute.

A good starting tempo would be half of what you'd be comfortable with if you were playing constant 16th notes. Ensure precise articulation of every note, and maintain a constant tempo throughout the task.

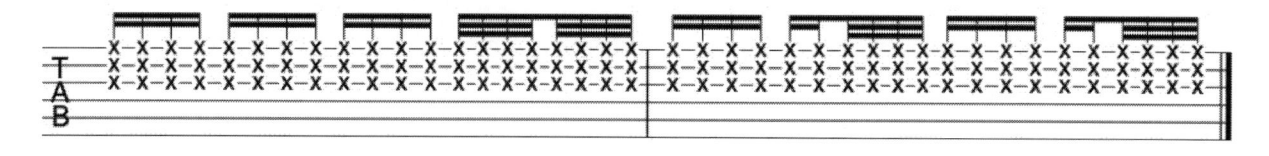

Chapter #9

A Few Fun Exercises

I play guitar because it lets me dream out loud.
— Michael Hedges.

Now that you have gone through all the tiring repetitive drills, let's end the book with a few fun musical exercises. You may look at these as more of musical compositions than exercises. I am sure you will enjoy it!

Have fun!

Vibin' In Detroit

Category: Picking Hand
Level: Beginner
Techniques: Strumming

Description: This simple Motown inspired chord progression could prove to be a feat in endurance. Remember: the right hand is the engine of the player, make sure to outline every 16th subdivision by hovering your picking hand above the strings over the rests, and make those ghost notes pop out!

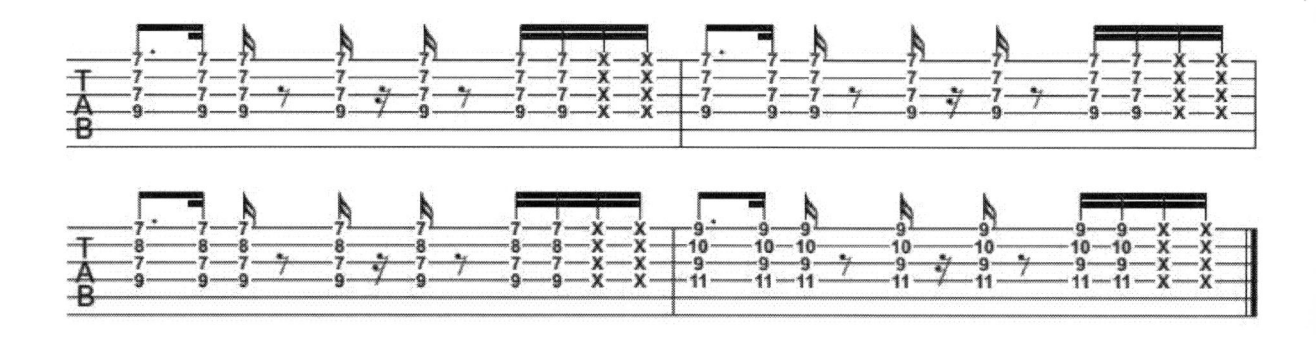

Impending Doom

Category: Picking Hand
Level: Beginner
Techniques: Downpicking

Description: A punishing 80s Thrash Metal riff constructed to obliterate your picking hand. Downpick every note, while maintaining a clear and percussive articulation. Even though it's an aggressive riff, try not to tense up and keep a relaxed wrist and pick grip.

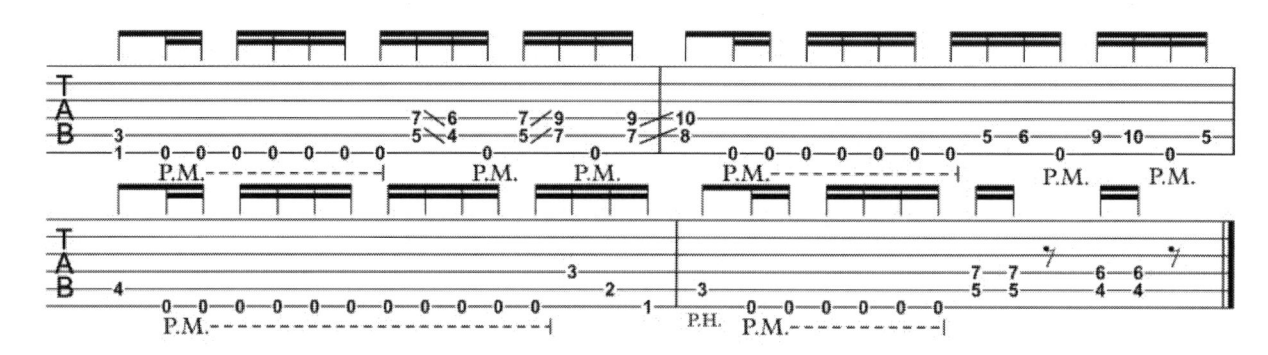

Chunky Riff

Category: Fretting & Picking Hand
Level: Intermediate
Techniques: Downpicking, Palm Muting

Description: an 80s reminiscent riff, optimal for training your downpicking and palm muting skills. Highlight the tonal differences between the more percussive muted parts and the resonant chords.

A

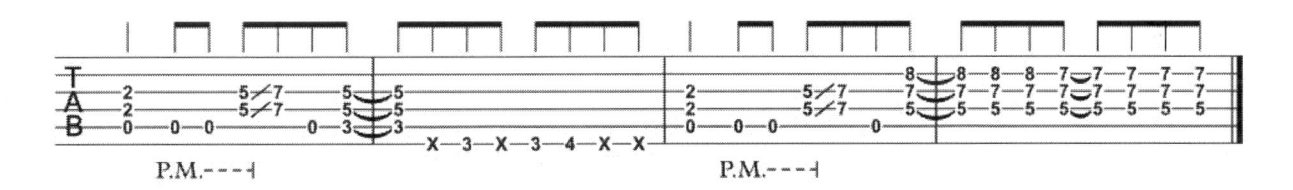

B

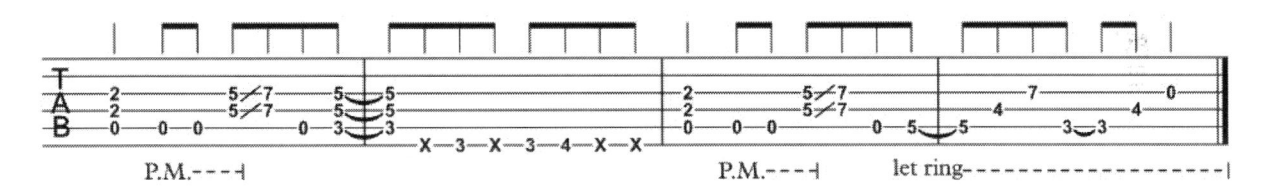

Picking Drill

Category: Picking Hand
Level: Intermediate
Techniques: Economy + Alternate Picking

Description: A folk flavoured rock riff, will do wonders for your picking technique. This could be approach in a number of ways, try to economise motion by always using a downstroke when ascending and an upstroke when descending, but be aware of how the pattern shifts and maybe incorporate alternate picking to rectify it before landing on the next 1.

A

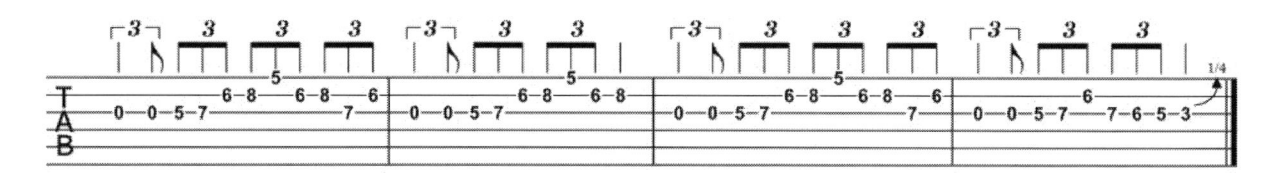

```
    ┌3┐  3    3    3   ┌3┐  3    3       ┌3┐  3    3    3   ┌3┐  3    3
                5              6—8      6—8        5              6—8      6—8        5              6—8      6—8        5              6                    1/4
T—0—0—5—7—————————————7———0—0—5—7———————————————0—0—5—7—————————————7———0—0—5—7———7—6—5—3
A
B
```

B

```
    ┌3┐  3    3    3   ┌3┐  3    3    3   ┌3┐  3    3    3    3    3    3    3
                    4—5              5—7              4—5    3—2              4—5              5—7     6—5    5
T—0—0—3—5—————0—5—7———0—0—3—5———0————5—3—0—0—3—5———0—5—7————————7———7—5—7—5————————5
A                                                                                                                          8—5—8
B
```

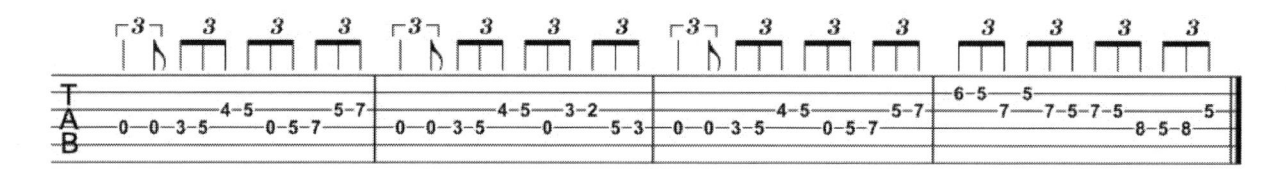

Oh, I Wonder

Category: Fretting & Picking Hand
Level: Advanced
Techniques: Two-Handed Tapping, Legato, Slide

Description: This odd-metered melodic line presents a variety of techniques to be employed, without having to pick a single note! Use the hammer-ons from nowhere technique to attack the notes with the left hand, and you index or middle finger to tap with your right hand.

Slides executed with the tapping finger can be tricky, make sure to master them at slower tempos before increasing it.

Chapter #9. A Few Fun Exercises

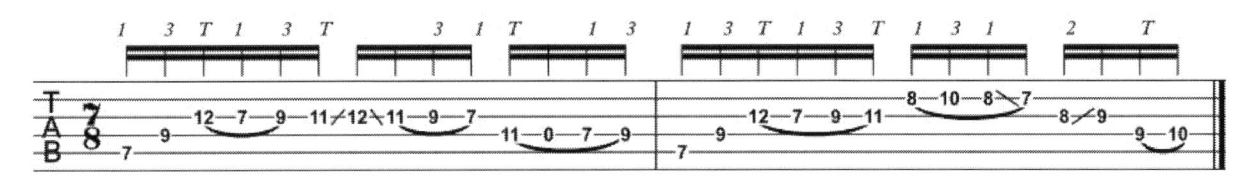

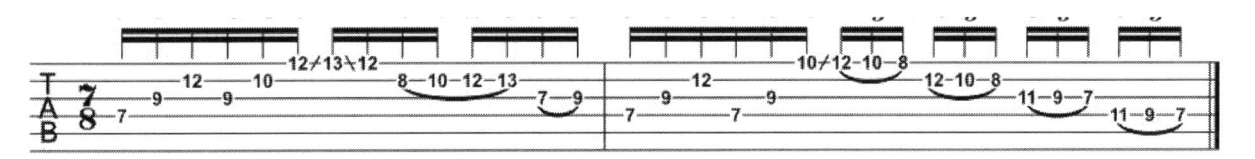

A

Until Next Time!

That brings us to the end of the book. I had a lot of fun writing the book and I hope it's same with you too. I hope I was able to add value and help your guitar playing. If yes, could you please leave a review for the book on amazon? Reviews are the lifeblood of books and I need as many as I can to reach as many people as possible.

Here's a link to leave a review:

http://bit.ly/guitarreview

Thank you again for selecting my book. Hope to see you soon with another book.

Like my Facebook page for fun guitar content.
Also, send me a video of you playing your favorite exercise from the book and I will feature it on the page.

www.facebook.com/theguitarhead/.

The End

Printed in Great Britain
by Amazon

MADLY MODERN QUILTS

Patterns and Techniques to Inspire Your Quilting Creativity

CAROLE LYLES SHAW

Quick & Easy Improvisational Blocks

Traditional Blocks Made Modern

Easy No Pin, No Template Curved Blocks

> Dedicated to Mildred Wilkins Lyles and Calvin William Lyles, my parents. Always with me...forever in my heart.

Madly Modern Quilts: Patterns and Techniques to Inspire Your Quilting Creativity.
©2016 Modern Quilter Media LLC. All Rights Reserved. Published by Modern Quilter Media LLC
1767 Lakewood Ranch Boulevard, #158
Bradenton FL 34211
www.modernquilter.us

The patterns in this book are copyrighted under U.S. copyright law and readers may use these designs for personal, non-commercial use. Commercial reproduction and sale is strictly prohibited. Patterns and quilt images are not to be copied or reproduced by any means whatsoever nor are they to be stored in electronic or mechanical information systems for any commercial use.

Quilt guilds and community groups using these patterns for Quilts of Valor™ and similar community service or charity projects are asked to request permission in advance to share patterns with group members and may make unlimited quilts for personal donation to Military Veterans, Active Duty Military and First Responders. Please credit Carole Lyles Shaw as the pattern designer on your label.

Available for purchase at:

www.CreateSpace.com/6008257

www.Amazon.com

www.MadlyModern.com

Note to Workshop Instructors (paid and volunteer): Workshop instructors are encouraged to use this book in classes while following the restrictions listed here. Please contact the author directly for permissions and/or information on discount bulk purchases so that you can provide a copy of the book or instructions to each workshop participant.

Thank you very much for respecting and protecting the author's intellectual property.

ISBN-10: 0-9907711-1-3

ISBN-13: 978-0-9907711-1-1

Credits
Graphic Design by Julie Lundy
  www.juliekaren.com
Quilt Photos by Brian James used with permission
  www.BrianJamesGallery.com
Longarm Quilting on selected quilts by Rose Ryan and Karlee Sandell
Special thanks to my wonderful workshop participants for your insight and support.

Disclaimer
We have made every effort to ensure the accuracy of the information in this publication. The information in this publication is provided in good faith, and Modern Quilter Media LLC assumes no responsibility for losses or damages incurred in using the materials, techniques, tools and instructions in this publication. No warranty is implied or given nor are any results guaranteed.

INTRODUCTION

TABLE OF CONTENTS

INTRODUCTION

WHAT IS A MODERN QUILT?	4
NEW TO MODERN QUILTING?	5
MODERN QUILT MYTHS	6
WHAT IS A FREEFORM PATTERN?	7
A WORD ABOUT SKILL LEVELS	7
MAKING A MODERN PATRIOTIC QUILT	7
RECOMMENDED SUPPLIES	8
USING A DESIGN WALL	9
ABOUT YARDAGE	10
SEAMS AND SEAM ALLOWANCES	10
SETTING SEAMS: STARCHING AND PRESSING	10
QUILT BACKING, BASTING AND QUILTING	11
PREWASHING FABRIC	11

PROJECTS

1	FRACTURED DISAPPEARING NINE PATCH QUILT	12
2	TROPICAL GARDEN QUILT	20
3	MODERN IMPROV RAIL FENCE QUILT	28
4	PARISIAN CURVES #1 QUILT	34
5	DISAPPEARING FOUR PATCH #1	40
6	DISAPPEARING THREE PATCH / FOUR PATCH QUILT	44
7	MARSALA IMPROV #1 QUILT	48
8	DISAPPEARING NINE PATCH WITH IMPROV BLOCKS	56
9	SPRING GARDEN DISAPPEARING NINE PATCH QUILT	60
10	LAYER CAKES AND RAIL FENCE IMPROV QUILT	72
11	FLAMINGO MINI QUILT	76

INTRODUCTION
WHAT IS A MODERN QUILT?

Let's start with the basic question: What makes a quilt modern? This is a question I often hear when talking with quilters I meet in local quilt shops, online or when I make presentations to guilds.

Modern quilting is a relatively new movement that has flexibility and innovation at its heart. Modern quilters build on and honor the many years of quilting tradition. But, don't worry about the "modern quilt police" showing up to squint at your quilt. The basic elements of modern quilt design are fairly straightforward. Modern quilting is a movement that is inclusive, open, welcoming and—most of all—*fun*!

The projects in this book were designed to introduce you to the elements of modern quilt design. Through completing these projects, you will learn how to use these design elements and then how to develop your own creative approaches to designing your own modern quilts.

Here is my list of modern design elements to look for when you wonder "What makes a quilt modern'?" You won't see *all* of these elements in a modern quilt, but the modern quilter usually has one or two (or more) of these elements in the quilt.

› *Simplicity and minimalism*

› *Modern traditionalism:* reinterpretations of the past (using traditional blocks in a new way)

› *Infinite edge:* no binding and no borders *or* making the binding and borders from the background fabric

› *Asymmetry and alternate grid layouts*

› *Use of negative space:* incorporating a background fabric that covers a noticeable percentage of the quilt top

› *Exaggerated or varied scale:* experimenting with block scale/size, such as making a quilt top that is just *one* large block floating in a lot of neutral space or making the same block in very different sizes in the quilt

› *Bold, modern graphics in print fabrics*

› *Modern color palettes*

› *Improvisation:* experimenting and playing with block design, quilt layout, fabric choices and all other aspects of the quilt design. Improvisation means seeing what emerges when you let go of pre-planning and measuring!

ONLINE RESOURCES

Please visit my website and my blog for more resources and updates on the projects in this book: www.madlymodernquilts.com or www.CaroleLylesShaw.com/My Books
Password to access additional materials: YmT3k9#!

NEW TO MODERN QUILTING? UPDATE YOUR STASH!

If you are relatively new to modern quilting, or if you have been quilting for a while, here are some tips to help you get started finding and using modern fabrics. You may already have a stash of traditional fabrics such as mid-30's reproductions, feed sack reproductions, batiks, civil war fabrics, traditional calicoes or other fabrics you've accumulated over the years. Or you might have picked up these fabrics at a guild auction or destash event.

Quilters are thrifty. We like to use what we have! You might be tempted to use your traditional fabrics in a modern quilt. Students sometimes bring a stash of these fabrics to my workshops instead of using modern fabric. I understand their impulse to "sew the stash". Unfortunately, my students have told me that they find it much more difficult to complete their modern quilt project because these fabrics don't have the same impact as the modern fabrics we can purchase today. They leave the workshop feeling less satisfied than the students who brought modern fabrics.

Before you start any of the projects in this book, I advise you to look through your stash and select *only* the most modern fabrics. Then, you may have to go fabric shopping at your local quilt shop--joy!!

Educate yourself about the many new fabric lines of prints, solids and even modern batiks offered today. If you're not sure what classifies as a "modern fabric", you can see many examples by checking online. Search "modern quilts" in your web browser. Look for quilts on Instagram™ and Pinterest™; search for the hashtag #modernquilt. Visit your local quilt shop and ask the owners to show you the most modern fabrics they have. Search the internet for "modern fabric quilt shops" to find what's current. Or visit my website Links page for a list of my favorite shops!

A final note about your stash: I occasionally find modern fabrics that I bought five or ten years ago hidden in my stash! Back then, I stumbled across these unusual 100% cotton fabrics in other sections of the fabric shop; they usually weren't with the quilting cottons. They appealed to me even though I didn't have a quilt project in mind at the time. Fortunately, between the quilting sections in local quilt shops and online stores, today we have hundreds of modern quilt fabrics at our fingertips.

MADLY MODERN QUILTS

MODERN QUILT MYTHS

Even though the modern quilt movement is just a few years old, it has been around long enough for quite a few myths to have developed. Here are a few things that, in my opinion, are *not* true about modern quilting:

› *Myth #1:* Modern quilters must use gray background fabric.

› *Myth #2:* At least 50% or more of a modern quilt must be negative space.

› *Myth #3:* Modern quilters do not hand piece, hand quilt or hand appliqué.

› *Myth #4:* Modern quilters never, ever use batik in their quilts. Modern quilters only use solids.

› *Myth #5:* Modern quilters don't bother to learn how to precision piece or match seams.

› *Myth #6:* Modern quilters don't make whole cloth quilts.

None of the above statements are true! If you look at the prize-winning quilts at QuiltCon, the annual conference of the The Modern Quilt Guild, then you will see quilts that break every one of these myths. (To see the QuiltCon prize winners, check the blog at www.themodernquiltguild.com)

One of the worst myths sounds something like this: "Modern quilters just do any old thing they want… they don't care about quality workmanship at all." This might be the most dangerous and damaging myth, because it labels modern quilters as too sloppy or lazy to learn how to make a quilt. The modern quilters I have met and talked with are dedicated to using the quilt construction techniques perfected by generations of quilters all over the world. When points are supposed to match, we try to make sure they match. We want our hand quilting or hand appliqué to look neat and in control. Whether we quilt on our home machine or longarm the quilt, we pay just as much attention to thread tension. Modern quilters make heirloom quality quilts every single day. Some of them choose to compete and win ribbons and prizes at Guild, Regional and International Shows and the rest of us applaud their craftsmanship.

However, modern quilters are not extreme perfectionists who obsess over tiny details that keep everyday quilters from actually finishing their quilts and using them on their beds. We want quilters to just get on with making the quilt. We learn from our mistakes when those mistakes get in the way of achieving the quilt that we set out to make. Yes, we reinvent the quilt design rules—while using best practices from our rich and diverse quilting traditions.

> "One of the worst myths sounds something like this: 'Modern quilters don't care about quality workmanship at all.'"

INTRODUCTION

WHAT IS A FREEFORM PATTERN?

I call these patterns *freeform* because they are guides with options; they can be adjusted and changed in many ways. For example, you can change the width and length of the borders if you want to make the quilt a different size. You can change the size of blocks to make them larger or smaller. You can add more negative space by adding blocks cut from background fabric.

> "Freeform patterns can be adjusted and changed in many ways."

You can easily change the way blocks are pieced or laid out. Don't worry about following the layout so precisely. For example, the Marsala Improv, Improv Rail Fence and Parisian Curves patterns in this book all allow lots of room for creativity.

Watch for boxes labeled "Freeform Tips" in the instructions. For some of the projects, I will provide alternate layouts to spark your creativity. Please send me pictures of your completed projects for my student work gallery on my website. I love to see how quilters use my patterns to make their own unique quilts. (And, please credit me on your label or when you post online. Thank you!)

A WORD ABOUT SKILL LEVELS

You won't see a skill level listed on the projects in this book. That's because I believe that any quilter can complete the projects in this book. If you've made a few quilts, then you can successfully complete these projects, too. I've had new quilters in my workshops make amazing quilts using the techniques and patterns in this book.

Don't be afraid to ask more experienced quilters for help if you feel uncertain. That's one reason new quilters join quilt guilds.

Remember, there are lots of free and paid quilt classes and tutorials online. Explore these offerings. They are relatively inexpensive or free, and you can watch them over and over to learn new techniques.

MAKING A MODERN PATRIOTIC QUILT

All of the patterns in this book can be used to make a modern patriotic quilt in your national colors. The trick is to select modern fabrics that bring freshness to the look. For more patriotic quilt patterns, check out my book, *Patriotic Modern Quilts* available on Amazon and at other outlets.

MADLY MODERN QUILTS

RECOMMENDED SUPPLIES

I recommend that you stock your sewing room with:

› *A rotary cutter and sharp blades:* Be sure to keep the inside of your rotary cutter clean. Lint buildup will affect your ability to cut accurately.

› *A standard cutting mat:* 18" x 36" is an ideal size if your cutting surface can accommodate it.

› *A rotating cutting mat:* I love my Olfa® turntable cutting mat. It allows me to spin a block around and make cuts without moving the fabric.

› *Rectangular rulers:* 6" x 12" and 6" x 24"

› *Square rulers:* These can be really helpful when you want to square up a block. I have several sizes ranging from 5½" to 15" square.

› *Thread for piecing:* I use yellow thread on top and gray in the bobbin. My favorite is So Fine!™ 50 weight by Superior Threads.

› *A sewing machine:* A standard home sewing machine that has straight stitch is all you really need, but if your sewing machine has built in stitches, such as a quilting stitch, try them out! Keep your machine oiled and dust free. Check your owner's manual for maintenance recommendations.

› *Sewing machine needles:* Change your needle frequently. I usually switch the needle after 20 hours of sewing *or* if I notice that the thread is tangling or something seems not quite right.

› *A ¼" foot:* Nearly all machines now have a ¼" or patchwork foot. Be sure to test the seam allowance. You might have to adjust your needle position to get an accurate ¼" seam.

› *Walking Foot:* This foot makes quilting *much* easier! You can sew straight lines, curves, spirals and circles with a walking foot. I also use it when I sew on the binding. There are wonderful tutorials online and in books about machine quilting.

› *Blue painter's tape or regular masking tape:* I use tape to mark quilting lines. I haven't had any problem with residue, but be sure to test the tape. *Never, never iron* the painter's tape or masking tape. This might cause the glue on it to become permanent. Use any brand.

› *STARCH: Best Press™ or Flatter™* I use these products instead of starch or sizing spray because I spray a lot and I don't want the build up you can get from starch. In this book, when I say STARCH--I am referring to these products.

I mark my quilting lines with blue painter's tape. I don't sew on or over the tape. When I get to an intersection, I lift the tape up and replace it if necessary.

INTRODUCTION

Testing block layouts for the Parisian Curves quilt on my design wall.

USING A DESIGN WALL

You will find it very helpful to use a design wall to make the projects in this book. Looking down at the quilt by placing blocks on the floor, or on a large table, isn't as effective as being able to see them on the wall. A design wall can be made inexpensively from a piece of white flannel, white cotton felt or cotton batting taped to a wall in your sewing room. You can also find oil cloth that has a flannel backing in the home decorating section of larger fabric stores. Oil cloth makes an excellent portable design wall because you can roll up your project without moving the blocks! It costs a bit more, but it's very helpful.

If you're fortunate enough to have a permanent sewing space, there are many inexpensive options for making a permanent design wall. I purchased lightweight foamcore or insulation panels at my local home improvement store and nailed them into the wall. I used thin nails to minimize the damage to the walls. Then, I pinned large pieces of white flannel to the panels. (You can also use batting or felt.) Most quilt blocks stick well to the batting, felt or flannel without pins. However, the panels I use are thick enough that I can easily use straight pins to hold my blocks. Test the panels by sticking in a straight pin before you purchase.

With a design wall, you will be able to see the quilt in its proper orientation. You can pin your quilt blocks to the wall and take photos of your progress. Move the blocks around when you are making an improvisational block or trying out ideas for your improvisational quilt layout. These photos can be really helpful in deciding which layouts look best. Take photos with your camera or camera phone and then view the image in black and white to check for good balance in value.

MADLY MODERN QUILTS

ABOUT YARDAGE

Yardage amounts assume that your fabric is at least 40" wide. Yardage estimates are generous for at least two reasons:

Improvisational changes: You'll be making improvisational changes to some—maybe even all—of these projects. I want to make sure you have enough fabric to experiment and try various options.

Backing fabric: Wait until your quilt top is finished to buy or piece the backing. Use the leftover fabric from the top to piece a backing. Take the large scraps and leftover blocks and randomly piece them together until the result is large enough for your project. You can always add other stash fabrics and even leftover blocks from other projects. Now you have a two-sided quilt!

SEAMS AND SEAM ALLOWANCES

Some of these patterns require a true ¼" seam allowance so that the block measurements are true. Some sewing machines, like my Janome 8900, have a built in ¼" seam stitch. However, even if your machine has a built in ¼" stitch, I suggest you sew a test seam on some scrap fabric and then measure the seam allowance with a ruler. You may find that you need to adjust the needle position to the right or left.

How to tell if your seam allowance is off: If you find that your blocks are coming out too small after piecing, the seam allowance may be off. If you change rulers or if you use your cutting mat to measure and also use rulers, double check that the measurements are all aligned.

When cutting your fabric, be careful where you place your rotary cutter—if you cut too far away from the ruler edge, then your cut pieces may end up too large. Even 1/16" can make a difference when added up across a large block.

SETTING SEAMS: STARCHING AND PRESSING

After I piece every seam, I lightly starch and press the block. I notice that my blocks lie flatter and I can match seams more easily when necessary. This is a vital step when making improvisationally pieced blocks. Frequent starching and ironing keeps the fabric from getting too wobbly when there are many bias edges. I use a light spray of BestPress™ (see the Recommended Supplies list.)

Tip: I say "starch"--but I use *Best Press*™. I spray the block or fabric and then wait about three seconds for the product to settle into the fabric. That helps avoid the shiny buildup that can occasionally happen. If you get some buildup, you can wash it out or use a slightly damp white cloth to brush it away.

INTRODUCTION

QUILT BACKING, BASTING AND QUILTING

Backing fabric: I have provided approximate yardage for backings but I suggest waiting until you finish the top before buying yardage for the backing. You will need less backing fabric if you use leftover scraps and yardage from making the top. Or for a really unique look, how about piecing the backing with those stashed traditional fabrics in the same colorway as the top? This will give you a completely different look.

Preparing Backing when using a longarm: Be very sure to check your longarm quilter's requirements, because usually the backing and batting must be several inches larger than the top.

Spray basting: There are quilt basting tutorials on the internet and in basic quilting books. I have a large design wall, so I pin my backing to the wall and spray it with 505™ Basting Spray. Then I put the batting on it, spray the batting and add the top. If the quilt is too large for my wall, I tape the backing on the floor and spray baste. I open windows and doors and turn on fans to ventilate the area when I use basting spray.

Quilting: I hope you will explore the many fine books and online tutorials and classes that teach modern machine quilting. Straight line quilting (sometimes called "matchstick quilting") is one of the popular options for modern quilts and can be accomplished on your home sewing machine. The lines can be pre-marked and very evenly spaced. Or, you can quilt straight lines random widths apart. Practice and see which method of straight line quilting is best for your project.

Of course, free motion quilting or using quilting stencils and templates are all good options. Remember, a modern quilt looks best when the quilting is also done with a modern approach.

PREWASHING FABRIC

I do not prewash my fabrics, but I always test them to see if they will run (or "bleed"). To conduct this test, cut a 2" x 2" swatch and wrap it in a piece of very wet white paper towel. Let the fabric and paper towel bundle sit for at least fifteen minutes before checking to see if the fabric runs. If it does, return it to the store immediately. In a humid climate, that dye could bleed when the quilt is stored away or washed.

In the picture below, the red fabric bled but the two blue fabrics did not. I threw away the red fabric because it was a few years old and I didn't know where I'd purchased it.

If the fabric seems to bleed only a little, you could try setting or washing out the excess dye. Wash the fabric with a product like ColorCatchers™, Synthrapol™ or Retayne™ and then test it again. (*Disclaimer:* I am not guaranteeing that these products will work.) If the fabric still bleeds, throw it away or return the yardage to the shop for a refund. Please don't give bad fabric away to another quilter.

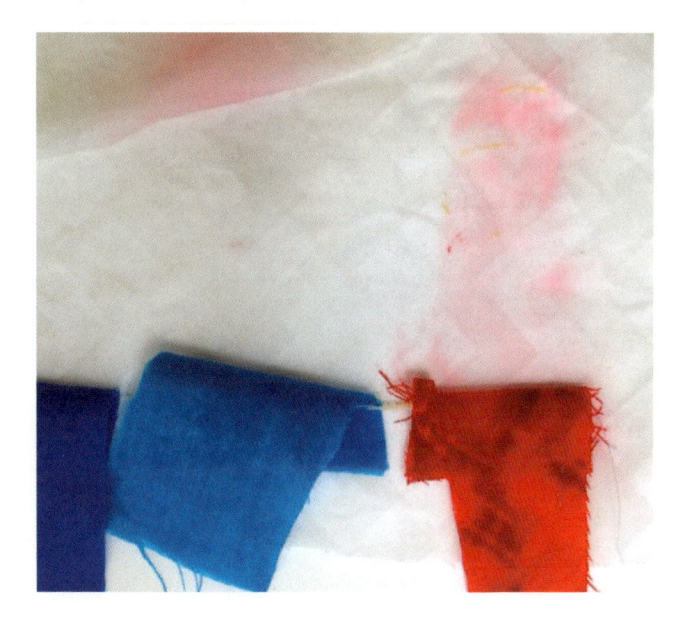

Blue fabric did not bleed. Red fabric bled onto the paper towel even after prewashing. I discarded the red fabric.

MADLY MODERN QUILTS

1 FRACTURED DISAPPEARING NINE PATCH QUILT

FINISHED SIZE: 60" x 65"

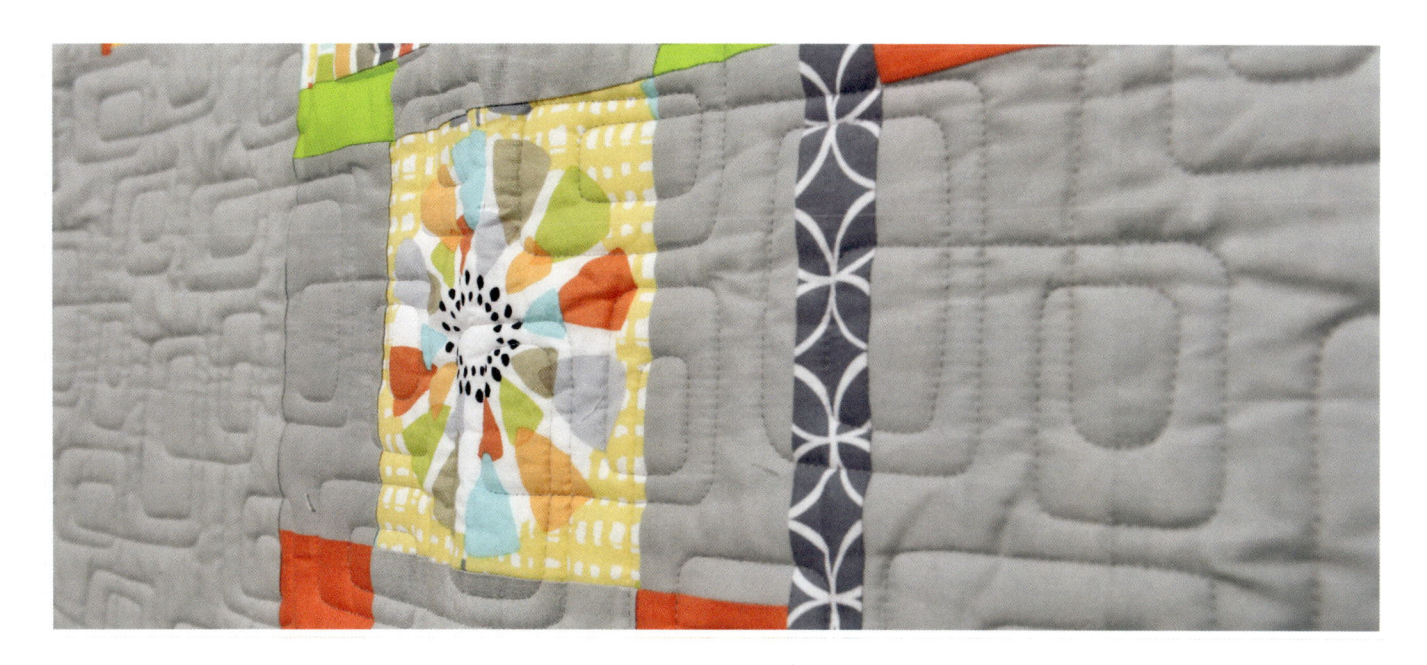

INTRODUCTION

This is an improvisational piecing project that will give you lots of opportunities to play and have fun! I call this improvisational process "fracturing" the block because I use a series of straight cuts to slice apart a large Nine Patch pieced block and then sew it back together. Eventually the original Nine Patch design disappears and an improvisational "fractured" block is what's left.

After you make your Fractured Blocks, you will construct a quilt center using five pieced blocks and four whole cloth blocks surrounded by asymmetrical borders. This is a very large Nine Patch so you are now playing with scale, which is a modern quilt design element.

Don't worry if you notice that your Fractured Blocks get smaller as you cut and rearrange them. I've suggested a starting size that will allow you to square up your blocks to the needed size after you finish fracturing.

You will use these modern quilting design elements:
› asymmetry
› modern traditionalism
› negative space
› alternate grid layout
› using a modern color palette
› playing with scale
› improvisation (the block fracturing is intuitive and unplanned—no measuring with rulers allowed).

MATERIALS LIST

Fabric estimates are generous, allowing sufficient print and solid scraps to start piecing a coordinated backing. Making a coordinated back is also a trend in modern quilting.

To make a quilt that is 60" x 65", you will need the following items. Items marked with an asterisk (*) should be cut as yardage, not a fat quarter:

› ½ yard of a bold modern focus fabric
  (select something with at least five colors in it)
› ¼ yard of coordinating print #1*
› ¼ yard of coordinating print #2*
› ¼ yard of coordinating solid #1*
› ¼ yard of coordinating solid #2*
› ¼ yard of coordinating solid #3*
› ¼ yard of coordinating solid #4*
› ¼ yard of one geometric print*
› ⅛ to ¼ yard of a stripe or geometric coordinating print to use for inserting strips*
  (You may need a bit more of this fabric depending on how you want to cut it for the inset strips. A long scrap may also work.)
› 5½ yards solid or tone-on-tone or other neutral for your background fabric
› *Backing fabric:* 4 yards
› *Batting:* 66" x 70"

MADLY MODERN QUILTS

GETTING STARTED: CREATING THE FIVE BASE BLOCKS

Start by making five Nine Patch Base Blocks, each measuring 22½" square. Each Base Block has nine 7½" squares.

Nine Patch Base Blocks use a different combination of your fabrics. It's important to use the background fabric in each Base Block so that the blocks blend into the background. In other words, you are drawing the negative space into the blocks themselves.

The Base Blocks are all oversized because you will be making several cuts into them. The cutting table shows how many squares to cut from each fabric.

FREEFORM TIP: FUSSY CUT!

You can fussy cut one of your 7½" squares to show off a special motif in your fabric. This example shows how it looks in a finished fractured block.

CUTTING TABLE

Fabric	Number of 7½" squares to cut
Background fabric *Gray in my sample*	12
Focus print *Option: you may want to fussy cut one or two of these blocks to feature a motif in the center.*	6
Coordinating Print #1	4
Coordinating Print #2	3
Solid #1	4
Solid #2	4
Solid #3	4
Solid #4	4
Geometric print	4

SPECIAL NOTE: ADDING A PIECED CURVE IN THE BASE BLOCK

You can add one or more curved blocks to the Base Block. When I fracture a Base Block that has a curved block, I only cut that block once because I want to preserve the curve as a strong visual element. In the example here, I *started* fracturing the Base Block by adding the gray and white diagonal strip. After that, I avoided cutting the curved block in the next fracturing steps. Don't worry! Once you start, you will quickly get the hang of it!

To make this block, start with two fabric squares that measure 9" square. For step-by-step instructions, see Parisian Curves p. 36. To see more examples of how I fracture a block, visit www.CaroleLylesShaw.com/MyBooks. Click on Additional Resources and use password YmT3k9#!

FRACTURED DISAPPEARING NINE PATCH QUILT

Step 1:
Cut the 7½" squares. See the cutting table for numbers of squares from each fabric. See "Special Note: Adding a Pieced Curve in the Base Block".

Step 2:
Arrange the 7½" squares into five Nine Patch Base Blocks. Keep it random so that each Base Block looks different.

> **FREEFORM TIP: REARRANGE**
>
> You can arrange the 45 squares into the five Nine Patch Base Blocks in any way you like. Make sure you have at least *three* background fabric squares and no more than two squares of any single color in each block. Make sure each Nine Patch layout is different, such as in the examples shown here.

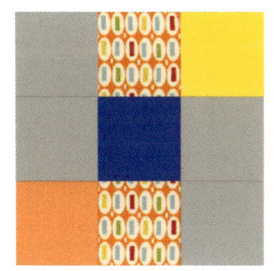

Step 3:
Sew the Nine Patch Base Blocks together. *(Yes, I make an effort to precisely match the points in my Base Blocks. Surprise!)*

HOW TO FRACTURE THE BASE BLOCKS

Taking one Nine Patch Base Block at a time, make a series of three to five fracturing cuts. In the following instructions, I'll show you several options for making the cuts. Remember, this is all about improvisation, not precise measuring or too much planning. There are several ways to make cuts and rearrange the pieces. You can make these cuts in *any* order.

To get started, read through the options in this section. Then select three or four of these fracturing cuts for your first Base Block. Be sure to step back after each cut and see what you like and don't like about the block. Your block will start to get smaller, so keep an eye on the size after you trim any "tails" off.

Cut 1
Cut the Nine Patch into three columns (Figure A). Move the middle column to the left side (Figure B) and sew the columns back together (Figure C).

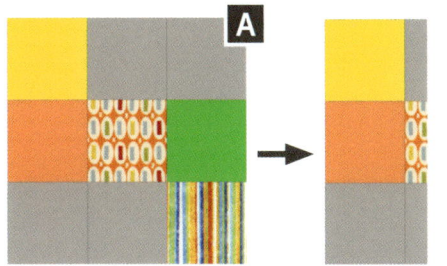

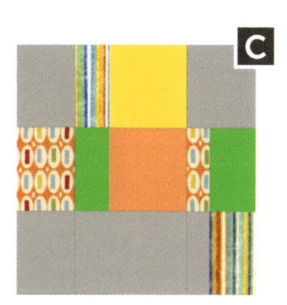

MADLY MODERN QUILTS

15

Cut 2

In this example, I used the block from Cut 1 to show you how fracturing can progress. In Figure A, I turned the block 90 degrees to the left. Now, make two cuts so that you have three rectangles (Figure B). Take one rectangle and cut it into two pieces with one horizontal cut, then rearrange the pieces (Figure C). Sew the pieces back together (Figure D).

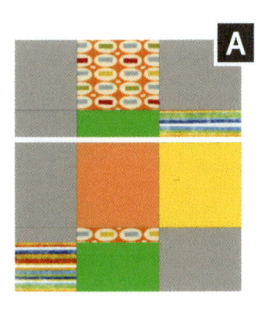

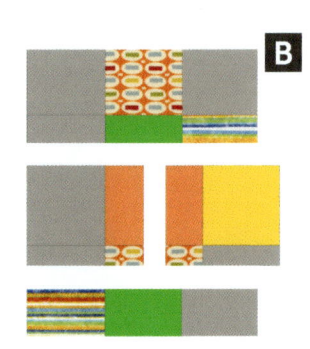

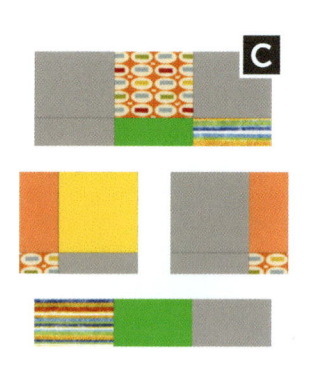

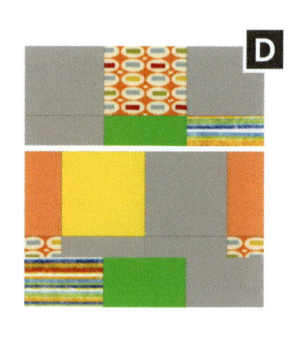

Cut 3

Select a Base Block. Cut off one skinny rectangle 2" wide (Figure A). Then turn the rectangle upside down and move it to the other side of the block (Figure B). Shift it up about 1½" so the seams do not match up. Sew the two pieces together (Figure C). After you sew one skinny rectangle back on, cut another skinny rectangle (Figure D). Shift this one and sew it back on (Figure E).

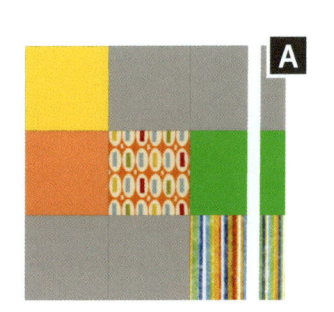

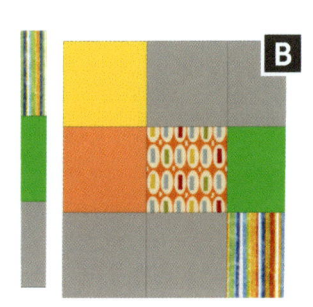

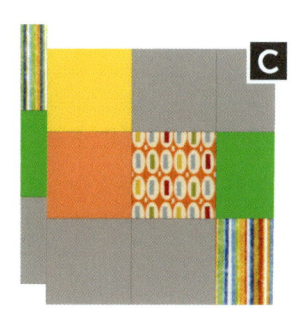

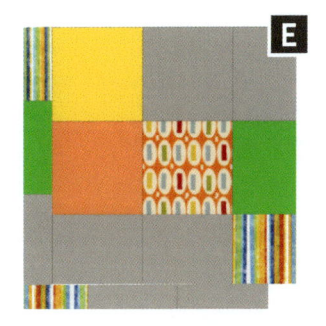

FREEFORM TIP: SAVE YOUR STRIPS

Save all those leftover trimmed off strips! You can use them in other Fractured Blocks or save them to create improv blocks to piece into the back.

FREEFORM TIP: MORE EXAMPLES ONLINE

To see more examples of how I fracture a block, visit www.CaroleLylesShaw.com/MyBooks. Click on Adidtional Resources and use password YmT3k9#!

FRACTURED DISAPPEARING NINE PATCH QUILT

Cut 4

Cut the original Base Block (Figure A) into four pieces by making one horizontal cut and one vertical cut (Figure B). Rearrange the pieces (Figure C) and sew them together (Figure D).

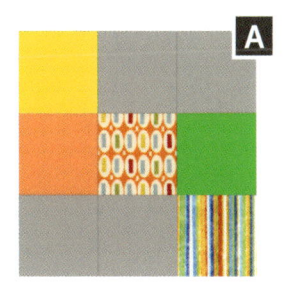

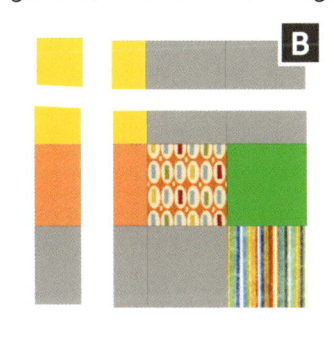

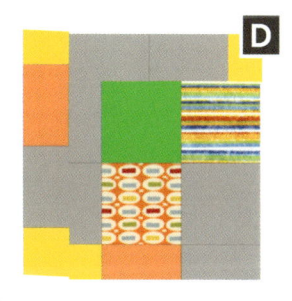

Cut 5: Adding Angles and Insets

In the sample quilt, you will notice that I made angled cuts and inset fabric strips. The fabric strips are 1" wide unpieced—do *not* add ½" to this measurement.

In this sample block, I cut one angle in the block, inserted the 1" wide striped fabric and sewed the pieces back together. I then cut a second angle and inserted the checked fabric. See A for how the block looks sewn together. This is only one possibility. You can make any type of angle cuts and insertions that you like. Usually, I am careful not to make the two angle cuts parallel to each other because that would be too regular. When you sew the angle pieces in, you will notice that the seams will *not* match up! That's a good thing because it will make the block more interesting.

> **TIP: MAKE A TURN**
> Every so often, before you make the next fracturing cut, turn the block 90° (a quarter turn). This will help you see more possibilities.

After inserting the angle strips, I continue fracturing using two or three of the other techniques in this section. In the samples here, I cut off one column measuring about 2" wide. (Figure B) Then, I moved the small strip to the other side of the larger piece, rotated the strip so it is upside down and sewed it into place. (Figure C) Now, the block looks *really* complicated!

Tip: Usually I trim the bottom strip and top overhanging strips. I save these pieces to use in other blocks.

After making 3 or 4 cuts, your block may be interesting enough that you are satisfied with it. Trim to size and put it up on the design wall. Take the next Base Block and start making cuts. Do not try to make the same cuts in each block. You may find that you have a certain cutting pattern. If so, try to vary cuts so that your blocks will look different from each other.

It's best to make one block at a time. If you make all five Fractured Blocks at once, you may find they turn out too similar!

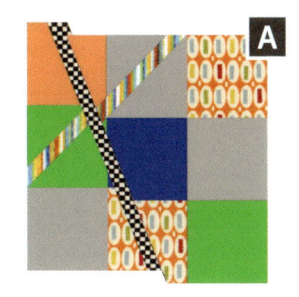

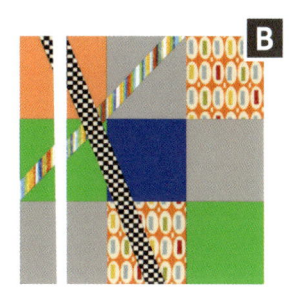

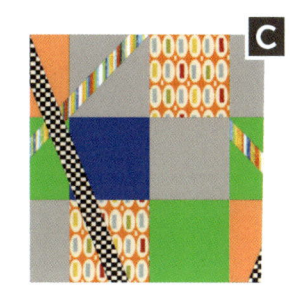

MADLY MODERN QUILTS

MORE FRACTURING TIPS

› When cutting the block apart, make sure each section is at least 1½" wide. If the sections get too thin, piecing them back together becomes difficult.

› Work on *one* Base Block at a time! Otherwise, you might get your pieces mixed up.

› Trim off any ragged or awkward edges as you go along. That way, you keep your block edges straight and this makes sewing them back together at each stage much easier. Don't square it up or measure it. Just give yourself a straight edge on to which you can sew the next piece.

› Starch and press lightly as you go, but don't stretch! I find that starching and pressing after each sewing step is really helpful because there are a lot of bias edges.

› Don't worry—seams will *not* match up when you start fracturing. In fact, if seams *do* start to match up, you need to break up those lines with some creative slicing and rearranging.

› You can't get this wrong! Play and have fun! These directions are general instructions. Use your own creativity to decide how to fracture your blocks. Experiment, have fun and don't over-think it!

COMPLETING THE TOP

1. Square up your five Fractured Blocks so that they measure 14½" square.

2. Cut four squares from your background fabric measuring 14½" square.

3. Assemble the center section as shown on the Assembly Diagram. You will have a large Nine Patch measuring 42½" square.

4. Refer to the Assembly Diagram. Make the following sections from the background fabric and add to the large center Nine Patch. (Be sure to measure before cutting in case your center is a slightly different size.)

    Sections F and H: 9½" x 42½"

    Section C: 9½" x 60½"

    Section G: 14½" x 60½"

TIP: IS YOUR BLOCK TOO SMALL?

If your fractured block is too small, you can easily make it larger by making an angled cut and inserting a rectangle of fabric.

For example, if my block is 13.25" x 14.75", I could insert a 1½" strip of fabric at an angle, sew together and measure the block again. Another option is to insert *two* strips at different angles for more interest. After inserting one or two angle strips, the block will be oversized and you can trim it down to 14½".

Another option is to sew on a leftover rectangle from another fractured block.

Do *not* try to measure a strip or other piece that will make your block come out to the right size. Follow your instincts and play!

This block has a featured center block that I cut carefully. I wanted to show off the flower graphic in the print fabric. When I fractured the block, I was careful to leave the center block alone.

FRACTURED DISAPPEARING NINE PATCH QUILT

ASSEMBLY DIAGRAM

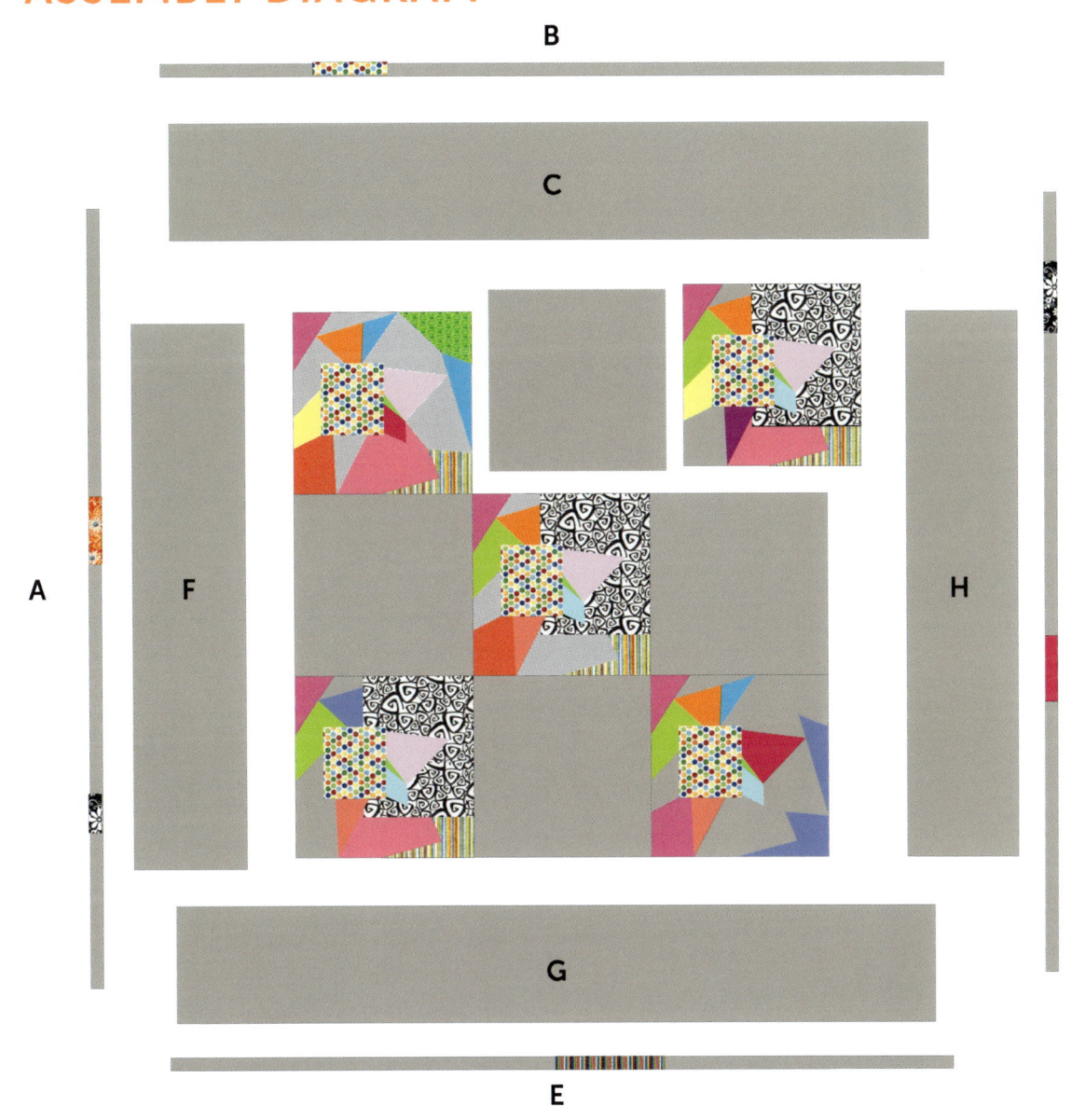

FINISHING AND BINDING

Assemble your quilt using the Assembly Diagram.

Backing: Piece a backing using leftover fabric and cut strips from the Fractured Blocks from the top. Need more fabric? Go to your stash! Modern pieced backings are often made with large cuts of fabric and orphan blocks pieced sufficiently large for the quilt dimensions. There is no pattern—just sew and measure until your backing is big enough.

Layering and basting: Measure the finished size of your top. Use batting that has at least 2" overlap on all four sides. If you are taking the quilt to a longarm quilter, check her or his requirements. Layer the top, batting and backing; then baste.

Quilting: Use your preferred method. Use straight line quilting for a modern look or use free-motion quilting designs or programmed designs.

Binding: Using background fabric and prints, make a binding with print fabrics randomly pieced as shown in sections A, B, D, E on layout.

MADLY MODERN QUILTS

2 TROPICAL GARDEN QUILT: SLOW CURVES AND STRAIGHT LINES

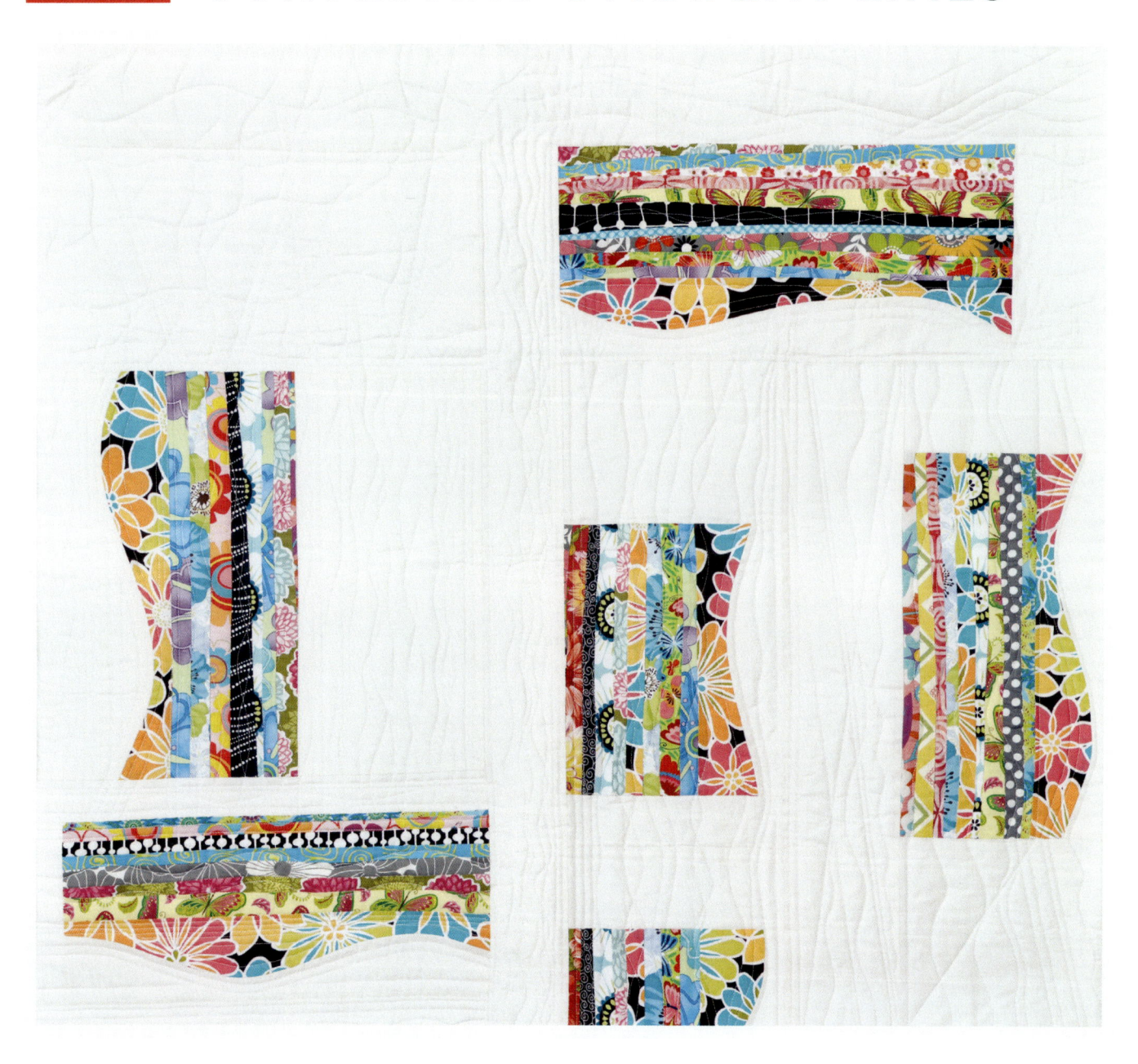

FINISHED SIZES:
WALL HANGING (OR BABY QUILT): 34" x 40"
LAP QUILT: 66" x 72"

INTRODUCTION

In making this quilt, you will use a wide variety of prints and batiks to create a unique lap quilt or wall hanging. This puts the "scrappy look" to use in a more modern setting. The freehand cut gentle curve adds movement and interest to your project.

It's easy to cut and piece the gentle curved blocks. I call them "slow curves"—gentle curves cut with a rotary cutter and pieced using a straight stitch. No pinning or precise matching is required. If this is your first time making curved piecing, I suggest that you practice on scrap fabric before cutting your project fabrics. There are many free video tutorials online—search for "piecing curves" or "piecing improvisational curves".

You will also improvisationally cut and piece skinny strips of multiple fabrics. The curved blocks and the strip blocks are then combined to make interesting rectangular blocks that are laid out in an improvisational design.

You will use these modern quilting design elements:
› use of negative space
› simplicity and minimalism
› asymmetry
› improvisation
› alternate grid layout
› use of a modern palette with bold fabrics.

You can make two sizes with these instructions. And, if you need to make it larger, you can easily customize the layout on your own.

MATERIALS LIST: WALL HANGING
FINISHED SIZE: 34" x 40"

› ½ yard of a multicolored bold modern print (this is your focus fabric)
› ¼ yard each of *four to six* coordinating prints. Aim for variation with interesting graphic designs that have diverse scale and colors. Go for modern designs in different scales—but don't go too small. Stand back a couple of feet from the fabric to see if the graphic design shows up or if it looks like a solid from a distance.
› ¼ yard of *one* black and white geometric print
› Two yards of a neutral fabric (gray, white or other color that will provide good contrast in the negative space. A tone-on-tone works very well.)
› *Backing fabric:* 1¾ yards
› *Batting:* 40" x 44"

MATERIALS LIST: LAP QUILT
FINISHED SIZE: 66" x 72"

› ¾ yard of a multicolored bold modern print (this is your focus fabric)
› ½ yard each of *six to eight* coordinating prints (or more). Aim for variation with interesting graphic designs that have diverse scale and colors. Go for modern designs in different scales—but don't go too small. Stand back a couple of feet from the fabric to see if the graphic design shows up or if it looks like a solid from a distance.
› ¾ yard of *one* black and white geometric print
› 4½ yards of a neutral fabric (gray, white or other color that will provide good contrast in the negative space. A tone-on-tone works well.)
› *Backing fabric:* 5½ yards
› *Batting:* 70" x 76"

MADLY MODERN QUILTS

CUTTING INSTRUCTIONS FOR SLOW CURVE BLOCKS

Here's how to cut and piece a curved block. This method requires no templates and no pinning.

Wall Hanging:

From the focus print, cut one rectangle measuring 6½" x 23". From the background fabric, cut one rectangle measuring 6½" x 23".

Lap Quilt:

From the focus print, cut one rectangle measuring 6½" x 20". From the background fabric, cut one rectangle measuring 6½" x 20".

These instructions are the same for both quilt sizes:

1. Place the two rectangles of fabric with *both* right sides up. This is very important because if you reverse them, the curves cannot be pieced together. In Figure 1 and 2, you see the white and the print rectangles. Before cutting, I put 1" wide painter's tape on *both* edges of the print fabric to keep my curve cutting within a boundary to maintain an ample seam allowance.

2. Place the rectangles on top of each other, both right sides facing *up*. The white fabric is underneath the print, and both fabrics have right sides facing up. Notice in Figure 2 that before I started cutting, I used another small piece of tape to hold the rectangles in place on my mat.

   Cut a very gentle curve using a rotary cutter which is small or medium in size. (Do not attempt to cut with scissors; you will not get a smooth curve.) Stay at least ½" away from the blue tape on the right and left side of your curve. After cutting, you will have four pieces of curved fabric. Take the top right hand curved strip and place it next to the bottom left hand curved strip, with both sides facing up. You will see that the curves match and the two pieces fit together. Then do the same with the two remaining pieces. You will have *two* matching pairs.

3. In Figure 3, you see one of the matching pairs ready for sewing. Make sure the curves mirror each other. Then, keeping them as aligned as possible, flip the print fabric over onto the white fabric.

TROPICAL GARDEN QUILT

4. With the right sides facing each other, match the top 1" (approximately) so that the two fabrics are aligned with the curve facing to your right. (See Figure 4). Sew on the curve using an approximate ¼" seam allowance. It is *not* critical to keep the seam allowance exactly ¼" wide. But try not to make it much wider, so that your curve will not become distorted.

5. After sewing, the strip will look wrinkly, as seen in Figure 5.

6. Gently press the strip flat, pressing the seam allowance to one side (Figure 6). The curve will magically flatten out!

   Tip: Use light steam or Best Press™ to make those curves behave. (Do not iron the seam open.) Notice that the bottom end will *not* match up. That means you've sewn it *correctly*. You will trim off the ends when you piece your curve with the other part of this block.

7. Trim the block to the needed *width only* referring to the cutting table on p. 25:
   › 3½" *wide* for wall hanging
   › 4½" *wide* for lap quilt
   You do not need to trim the length yet.

TIP: PRACTICE MAKES PERFECT

Practice! If you have never pieced a gentle curve, then practice first with scrap fabric. You can *gently* ease the fabric into place as you sew to make the curves "fit" because you can iron it flat using Best Press™ or light steam. Don't pull the fabric; ease it gently as you sew. Watching tutorials really helped me get started, but practicing with scrap fabric made all the difference. Even now, if I haven't sewn a curve for a while, I practice before cutting my good fabric.

MADLY MODERN QUILTS

CUTTING AND ASSEMBLING THE STRAIGHT LINE BLOCKS

These are simple "rail fence" blocks. Start by cutting each print fabric in strips measuring as follows:

Wallhanging
- ¾" x 20"
- 1" x 20"
- 1¼" x 20"
- 1½" x 20"

Lap Quilt
- ¾" x 22"
- 1" x 22"
- 1¼" x 22"
- 1½" x 22"

You will need between four and eight strips for each block depending on the block width of your strips. (Refer to cutting chart to determine how wide to make each rail fence block.)

Piece straight strips together (Figure A). Be sure to mix up the colors and fabrics in each block to achieve an improvisational look. Try to place different colors next to each other. Try *not* to use the exact same fabrics in each block to add interest.

If your seams are a bit off, do *not* take them apart. A bit of crookedness adds more interest.

ASSEMBLING THE PRINT BLOCKS

Sew one curved block to each straight line block (Figure B). Notice that curve block is a slightly different length. Trim to size according to the cutting table (Figure C).

See the block size charts and layouts or the recommended sizes for print and background fabric blocks. Remember—this is an improvisational quilt and you can change the sizes and locations of the blocks to create a unique layout.

FREEFORM TIP: VARY LENGTHS AND WIDTHS

You can make the pieced blocks in different lengths and widths. For example, suppose you run out of rail fence sections. You could cut block P1/P2 so that it measures 15½" long instead of 20½". Then, you change block O to measure 17½" x 16½".

TROPICAL GARDEN QUILT

CUTTING TABLE: WALL HANGING

34" x 40"

(These are unfinished block sizes.)

Block	Size (")	Block	Size (")
A	40½ x 2½	K2	4½ x 11½
B	6½ x 17½	L	3½ x 16½
C	2½ x 16½	M1	3½ x 16½
D1	3½ x 16½	M2	6½ x 16½
D2	5½ x 16½	N	1½ x 17½
E	7½ x 16½	O	1½ x 6½
F	4½ x 34½	P1	3½ x 16½
G1	3½ x 17½	P2	3½ x 16½
G2	3½ x 17½	Q	5½ x 17½
H	2½ x 6½	R	5½ x 7½
I	4½ x 19½	S1	3½ x 5½
J	3½ x 7½	S2	4½ x 5½
K1	3½ x 11½	T	8½ x 12½

CUTTING TABLE: LAP QUILT

66" x 72"

(These are unfinished block sizes.)

Block	Size (")	Block	Size (")
A1	10½ x 10½	N	2½ x 20½
A2	4½ x 10½	O	12½ x 16½
B	14½ x 10½	P1	20½ x 10½
C	6½ x 63½	P2	4½ x 20½
D	28½ x 6½	Q	8½ x 32½
E	4½ x 32½	R	13½ x 14½
F1	4½ x 14½	S1	9½ x 15½
F2	10½ x 14½	S2	4½ x 15½
G	14½ x 8½	T	5½ x 29½
H1	10½ x 10½	U1	10½ x 18½
H2	4½ x 10½	U2	4½ x 18½
I	10½ x 32½	V	14½ x 11½
J	28½ x 2½	W	32½ x 10½
K	8½ x 11½	X1	20½ x 9½
L1	7½ x 20½	X2	4½ x 9½
L2	4½ x 20½	Y	9½ x 14½
M	28½ x 11½		

MADLY MODERN QUILTS

ASSEMBLY DIAGRAM: WALL HANGING

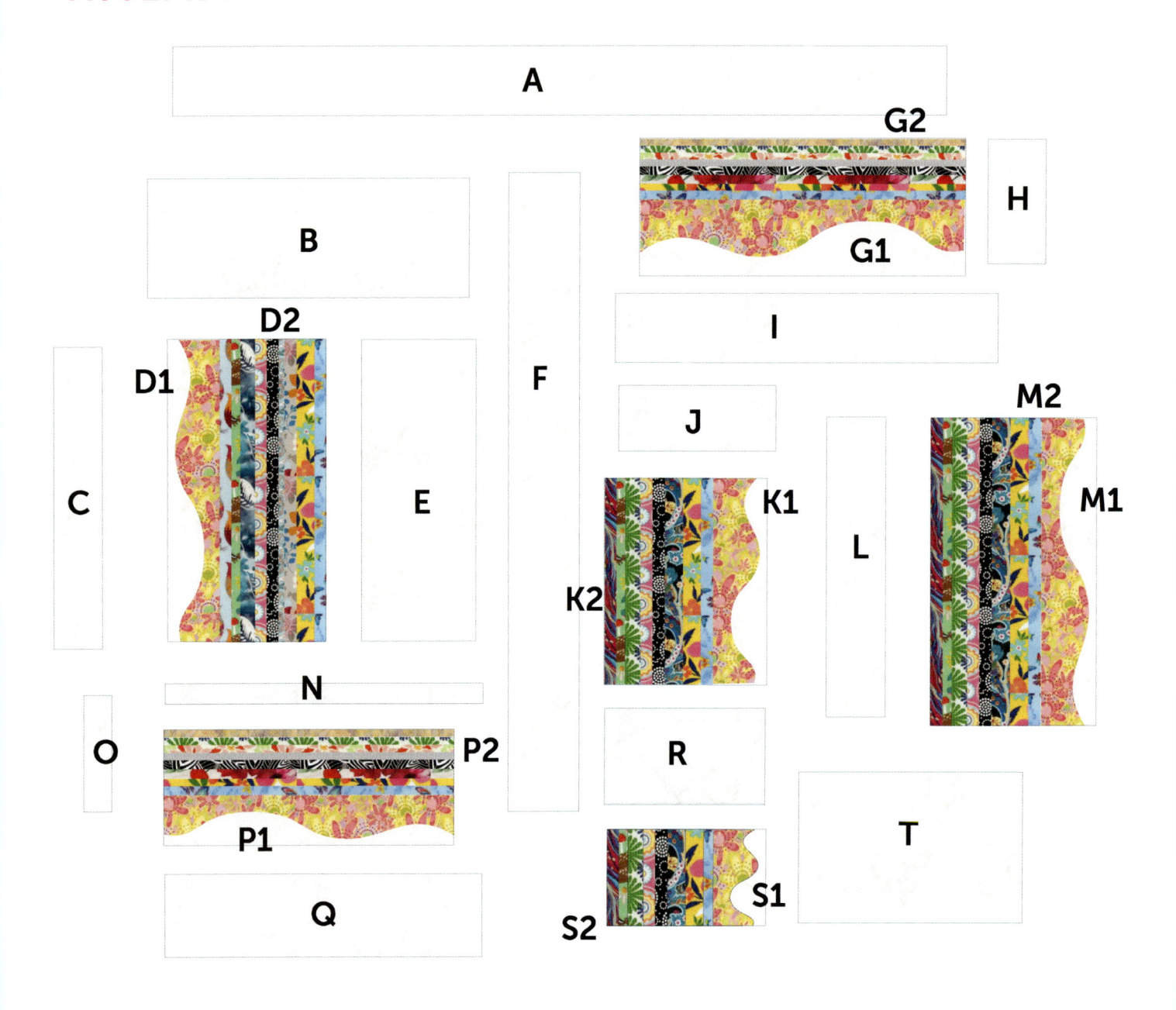

FINISHING AND BINDING

Assemble your quilt using the Assembly Diagram.

Layering, basting and quilting: Layer the quilt top, backing and batting. Then baste and quilt as desired. I recommend straight line quilting using a thread color that blends into your background fabric. I also suggest adding occasional lines of quilting echoing the curves using a contrasting color (variegated, bold or subtle—it's your choice!)

Binding: Create a binding using leftover background fabric with randomly sized sections of the other fabrics. This is improvisational, so the choice of fabric and placement is up to you.

TROPICAL GARDEN QUILT

ASSEMBLY DIAGRAM: LAP QUILT

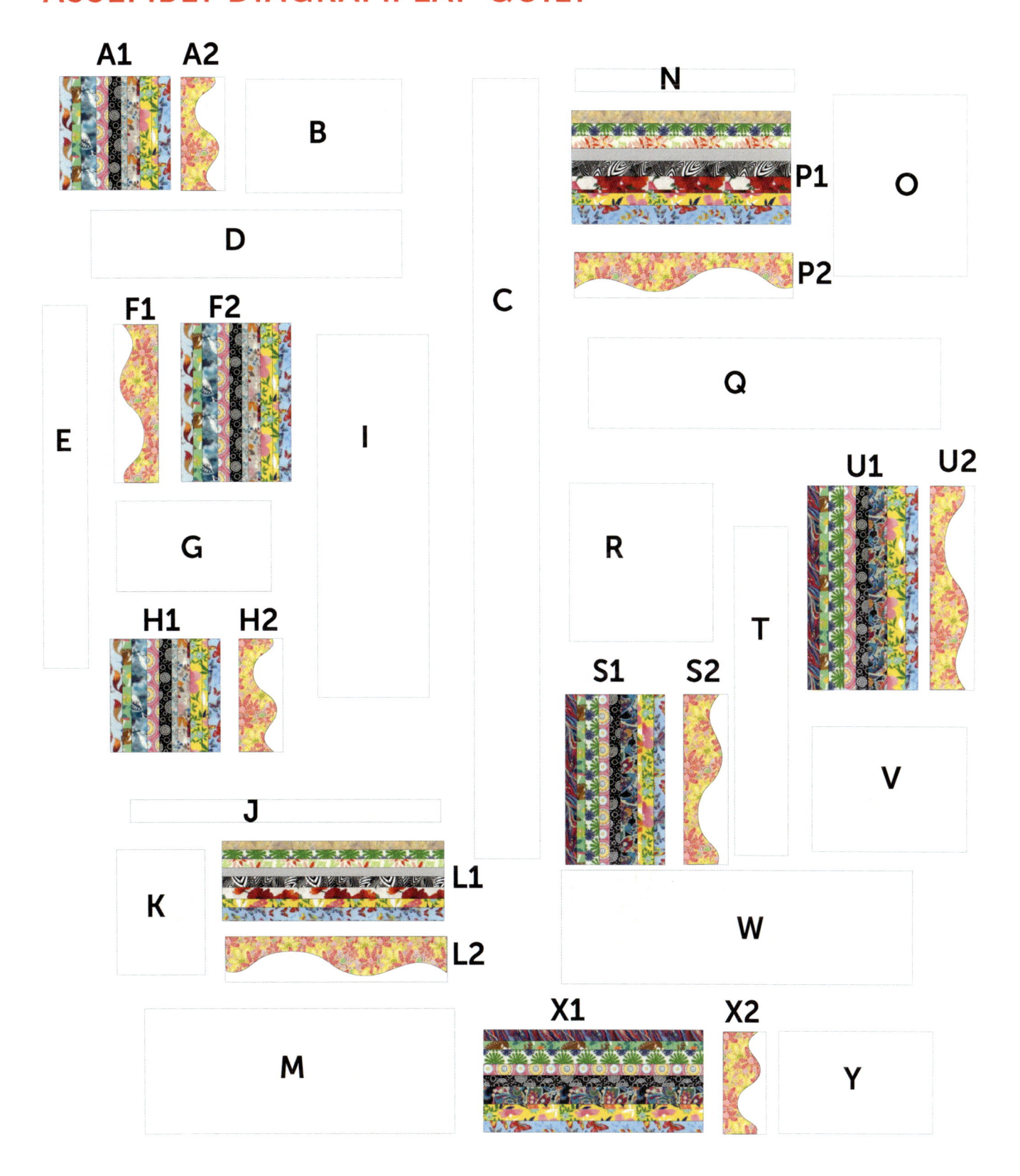

MADLY MODERN QUILTS

27

3 MODERN IMPROV RAIL FENCE QUILT

FINISHED SIZE: 61" x 67"

INTRODUCTION

This is an improvisational piecing project that will give you lots of opportunity to play and have fun! The quilt is made with pieced rail fence blocks and large solid areas. You will piece rail fence blocks first. Then you will cut blocks from the rail fences and the solid fabrics.

This example uses patriotic fabrics but you can choose any set of coordinating prints and solids. I've also provided other fabric and color choices in these instructions.

You will use these modern quilting design elements:

› asymmetry
› use of negative space
› alternate grid layout
› improvisation.

FREEFORM TIP

Notice that some of the rail fence blocks are horizontal and others are vertical in the Assembly Diagram. You can follow this layout or mix them up in any way that you like. It's important to mix up the orientation to keep it interesting.

TIPS FOR CHOOSING PRINT FABRICS

1. See page 32 for ideas on other fabric combinations.
2. Start by choosing a "focus print" that has several colors in it. Check the selvedge color dots and use them to guide your other fabric choices.
3. Go for modern designs in a variety of scales—but don't go too small. Stand back a couple of feet from the fabric to see if the graphic design shows up or if it looks like a solid from a distance.
4. Graphic prints (such as wavy stripes, bold polka dots and text fabrics) work well in this quilt. Print fabrics should be bright and busy!

MATERIALS LIST

To make the quilt top, you will need:

› *Background fabric:* 4½ yards of one solid neutral (tone-on-tone highly recommended). In the sample this is blue fabric.
› *For accent fabric:* 1½ yards of a second solid color (tone-on-tone highly recommended). In sample quilt, this is the solid red fabric.
› *For rail fence blocks:* ⅜ yard each of six to nine different modern prints.
› *Backing fabric:* 4 yards
› *Batting:* 64 x 70"

ADDITIONAL ASSEMBLY INSTRUCTIONS

AVAILABLE ONLINE

Please visit www.CaroleLylesShaw.com/My Books. For additional directions for assembling this quilt, download Modern Improv Rail Fence Quilt Assembly, use password YmT3k9#!

MADLY MODERN QUILTS

CUTTING TABLE: RAIL FENCE BLOCKS

This table gives you the sizes you need for the rail fence blocks. Some blocks have strips that are arranged horizontally; others are arranged vertically. As you cut each block, you will decide on the orientation according to your own taste.

Step 1

Cut the print fabrics into strips measuring approximately 1" wide, 1½" wide and 2" wide by 20" long.

Step 2

Sew the strips together randomly into sets that are approximately 10" wide. Make at least four of these sets to begin with. Make sure the sets look different—don't use the same fabrics in the same sequence for each block. Mix it up for a scrappy look.

Step 3

Cut sixteen rail fence blocks in sizes according to the table below.

Rail Fence Block #	Size (")	Block #	Size (")
1	6½ x 7½	11	7½ x 5½
2	5½ x 5½	12	4½ x 5½
3	5½ x 5½	13	3½ x 11½
4	2½ x 5½	14	5½ x 6½
5	5½ x 5½	15	3½ x 6½
6	5½ x 7½	16	2½ x 8½
7	2½ x 8½		
8	5½ x 8½		
9	5½ x 3½		
10	5½ x 8½		

CUTTING TABLE: BACKGROUND BLOCKS

The remaining blocks are cut from your background and accent fabrics. The block sizes are in the table below. To make it easier to follow the sample quilt, I labeled the "red" blocks in the table. *All* of the other blocks in the table are cut from the blue background fabric. Red is the accent fabric in my quilt. Write in your own color names to make it easier to keep track as you follow the cutting table.

Block #	Size (")	Block #	Size (")	Block #	Size (")
A	7½ x 8½	Q	2½ x 8½	GG	7½ x 5½
B red	1½ x 6½	R red	8½ x 8½	HH	11½ x 8½
C	38½ x 8½	S	5½ x 8½	II	3½ x 5½
D red	4½ x 8½	T red	2½ x 7½	JJ red	2½ x 7½
E	4½ x 8½	U	8½ x 7½	KK	8½ x 11½
F	8½ x 60½	V	5½ x 8½	LL	11½ x 6½
G	5½ x 9½	W red	1½ x 8½	MM red	7½ x 6½
H	2½ x 10½	X	7½ x 8½	NN	3½ x 6½
I red	5½ x 5½	Y	10½ x 8½	OO	3½ x 6½
J red	2½ x 10½	Z	15½ x 8½	PP	7½ x 6½
K red	2½ x 5½	AA	7½ x 60½	QQ	9½ x 5½
L red	2½ x 7½	BB	7½ x 18½	RR red	9½ x 2½
M	8½ x 7½	CC red	2½ x 3½	SS red	5½ x 3½
N	3½ x 5½	DD	7½ x 5½	TT	4½ x 3½
O	3½ x 5½	EE	6½ x 8½	UU	6½ x 6½
P	2½ x 5½	FF red	7½ x 2½	VV	18½ x 6½
				WW	13½ x 60½

MODERN IMPROV RAIL FENCE QUILT

ASSEMBLY DIAGRAM

More information--www.CaroleLylesShaw.com/MyBooks. Click on Adidtional Resources and use password YmT3k9#!

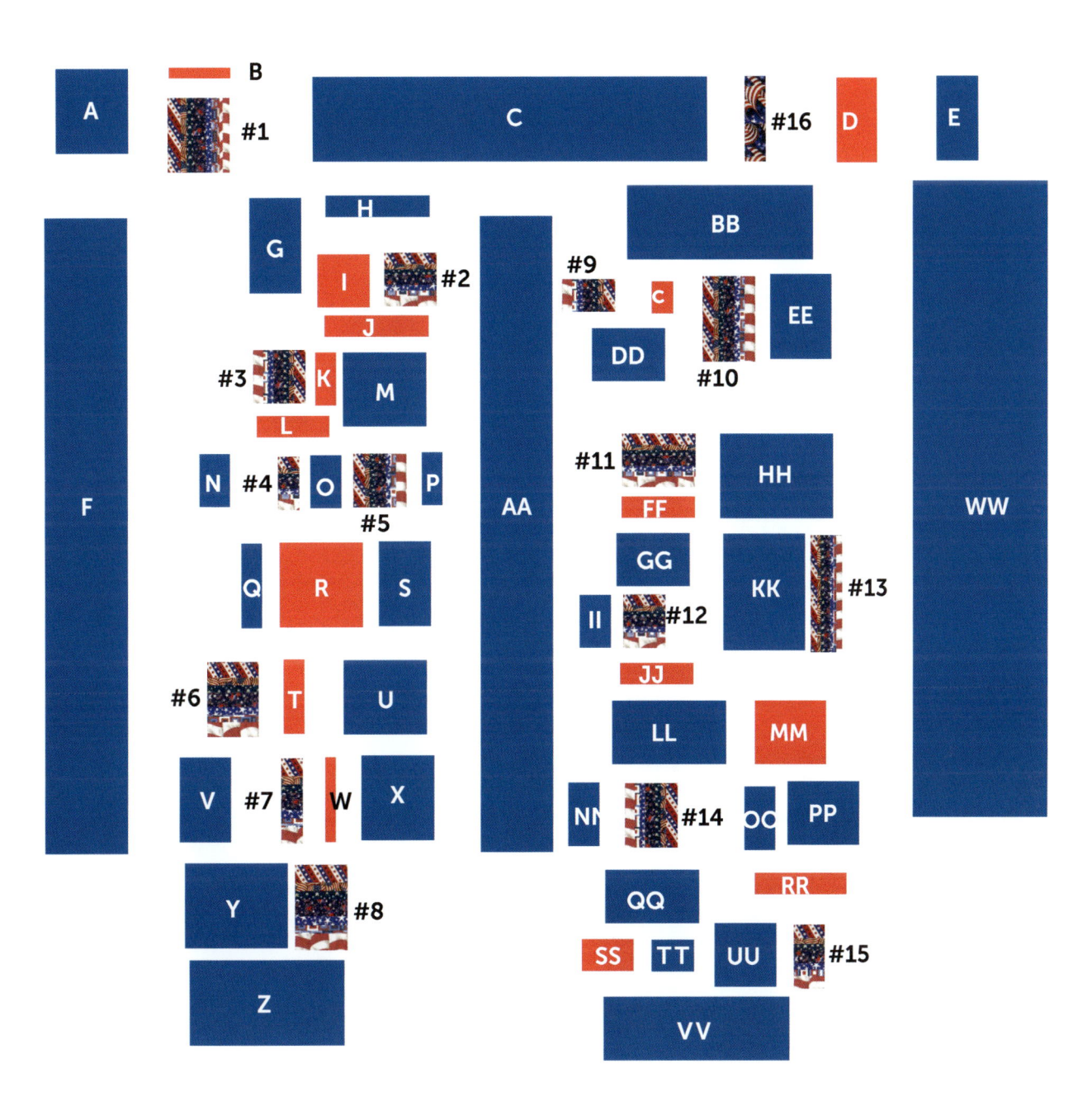

FINISHING AND BINDING

Assemble your quilt using the Assembly Diagram.

Layering, basting, quilting and binding: Layer the quilt top, backing and batting. Then baste and quilt as desired. I recommend straight line quilting using a thread color that blends into your background fabric. You can add occasional lines of quilting using a contrasting color. Bind the quilt using your preferred style.

MADLY MODERN QUILTS

FREEFORM TIP: In the sample quilt, I added rail fence blocks to border block F. You could do the same with Border block WW. If you want to make the quilt larger, add additional borders to the top and bottom of the quilt or add larger borders to the sides. You can leave these borders plain or add rail fence or solid accent blocks to the borders. For example, to add a finished 5" wide border on all four sides, you will need 1¾ yards of fabric.

ALTERNATIVE FABRICS AND COLORS

This is a very versatile pattern! You can use leftover yardage from other projects to make the rail fence blocks (as long as the scraps are long enough). Here are some examples of alternative colors and fabrics you can use to make this quilt. There is a blank template on the next page to help you plan your quilt.

Figure A: For the rail fence blocks: The floral on the far right is the focus fabric. I then selected a lilac, purple, two black and white prints and a grunge pink. The gray fabric on the far left will be used as background fabric.

Figure B: For this option, I selected a darker modern print as background fabric (far left). It has a similar color way: the taupe background is a deeper version of the pale taupes and beiges. And, it has vibrant modern turquoise markings—there is turquoise in some of the other prints. This fabric will create high contrast between the rail fence blocks and the background.

Figure C: In this final example, I selected low volume fabrics, some of which have a Parisian theme. The pale batik on the far left will be used as the background fabric to create negative space. Overall, this will be a very low contrast quilt—a change from my usual very bright palette.

Figure D: I changed the background fabric to a mid-tone gray with orange dots to give more contrast.

PLANNING YOUR QUILT

Ready to start planning your own quilt? Copy the template on this page. It's the layout for this quilt. Use colored pencils or cut small pieces of fabric and glue them down to see how the colors might work.

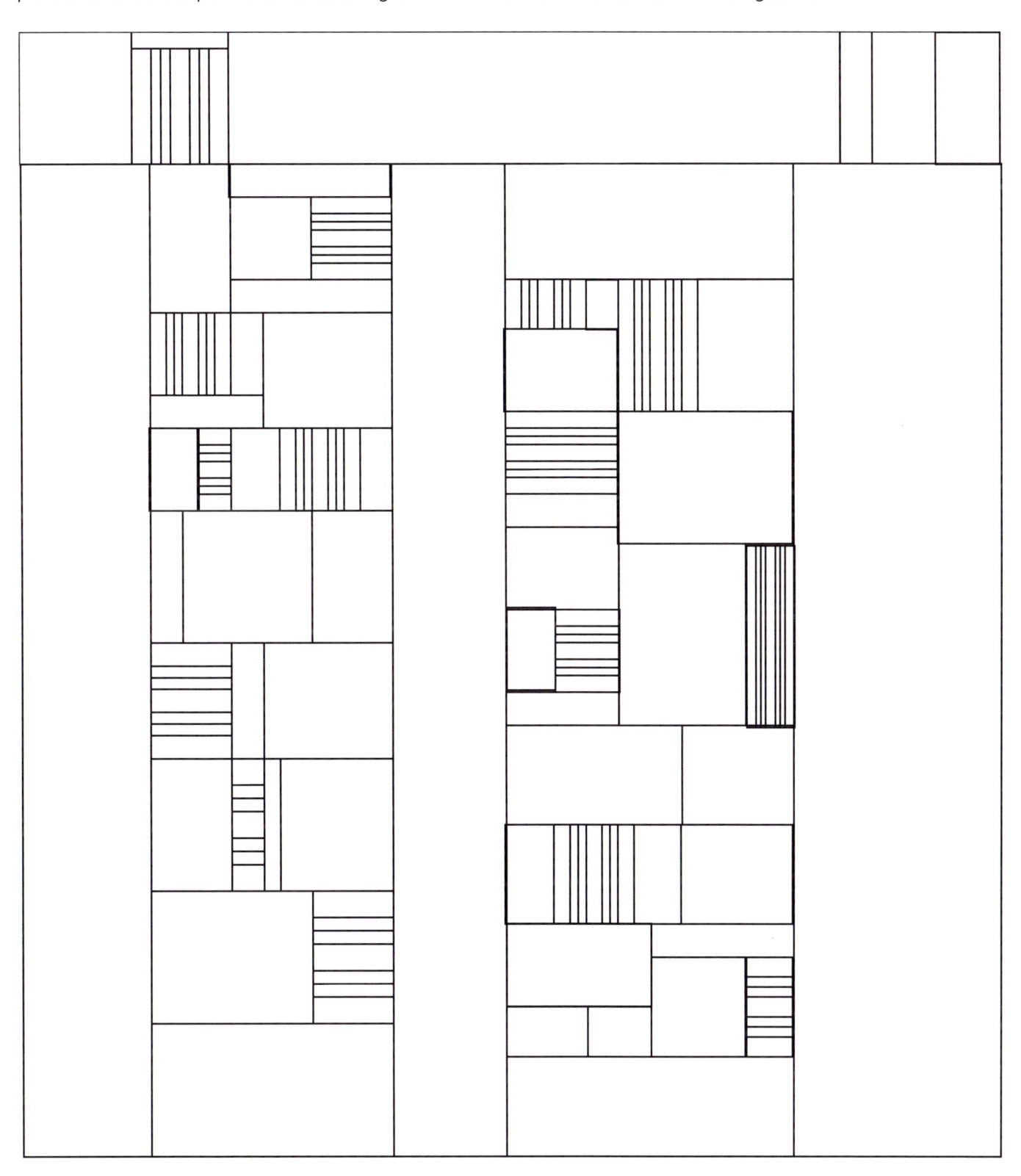

MADLY MODERN QUILTS

33

4 PARISIAN CURVES #1 QUILT

FINISHED SIZE: 34" x 56"
(INCLUDES INSTRUCTIONS FOR MAKING THE QUILT LARGER)

34 PARISIAN CURVES #1 QUILT

INTRODUCTION

This is a quilt created using just a few block sizes that fit together easily. The freehand cut curves make the quilt look very improvisational. You will combine the curved blocks with blocks cut from the background fabric for a planned layout that looks completely improvised. This project will give you practice cutting and piecing improvisational curved blocks, combining prints and solid fabrics, alternate grid layout and incorporating negative space.

You will use these modern quilting design elements:
- Improvisation
- Varied block sizes (varied scale)
- Alternate grid layout
- Use of negative space

MATERIALS LIST

I call this quilt Parisian Curves because I used a Paris themed print fabric in my first quilt based on this pattern. The Paris fabric and a bold floral were my two focus fabrics. The floral guided my color choices because the Paris fabric had a very neutral palette.

Make sure you have contrast in your choices. Lay out the fabrics and stand back. Is there a value change? Is there variety or do all the prints look similar? You want to make sure the curves stand out when you put fabrics next to each other.

These are suggested fabric choices—you can pick any combination that appeals to you.

To make a quilt measuring 34" x 56":
- ½ yard each of one or two focus prints. I usually use *one* very bold and bright print and one more neutral. I use these fabrics to guide my color choices when I select remaining solids and prints. (The Paris fabric is very hard to find. Just pick an interesting novelty print that *you* like.)
- Fat quarters of at least five coordinating solids. Select light, medium and dark solids.
- Fat quarters of at least six varied but coordinating prints. Look for variety especially in scale of the print. Look for light, medium and dark values. A stripe is a nice choice for getting variety in the look.
- Optional Fat Quarter of one or two black and white prints or another geometric print with an interesting graphic design.
- 4 yards neutral fabric for your background. This can be a solid, tone-on-tone or a very low volume print. In this quilt, I used a mottled gray Moda Grunge fabric.
- *Batting:* 38" x 60"
- *Backing:* 3¼ yards

NOTE ABOUT USING BATIKS
I love batik fabrics and like throwing in one or two in a project like this. They tend to read as solids unless they have a contrasting print or a variety of colors in them.

MADLY MODERN QUILTS

STEP 1: MAKING CURVED BLOCKS A, F, J

This is an improvisational process. The key is to make sure that each piece of fabric you are adding is large enough to leave plenty of space for cutting. See the sample photos for an example of the process.

Begin by cutting one background square measuring 11" square. Next, cut one 11" square from a print or solid. Place the two squares with *both* right sides facing *up*. Cut a gentle freehand curve. You now have four pieces—two backgrounds and two prints. Sew one background curved piece to the print or solid piece. (Save the remaining two pieces to use in other curved blocks.)

For this example, I started with a solid square and added one of the volume prints. Notice in the sample quilt that I varied the number of curves that I cut and pieced to make each block. Some blocks have only two fabrics. Others have three or four fabrics. This adds variety to the blocks.

1. First, I placed the two squares *right side up* and cut a gentle arc or curve from the top right to the bottom with my rotary cutter. I had four pieces and I selected one inner piece and one outer piece for this block. In Figure 1 you see two curved pieces ready for sewing.

2. Place the two pieces right sides together. Gently and slowly sew approximately ¼" from the edge of the curve. Stop every four or five stitches to re-adjust the fabric and keep the edges together. Do not pin. (See Figure 2).

3. Your first curve block is ready for gentle pressing. I pressed the seam towards the darker fabric in Figure 3.

4. I decided to add another fabric: a bright floral. I selected a small square—large enough to cover the area so I could piece it easily (Figure 4).

PARISIAN CURVES #1 QUILT

5. I placed the floral print on top, right sides facing up and cut a new curve (Photo 5). Now I will sew the new curve to the block. *Do not trim any ends or square it up.*

6. I added a third print to this block to add more graphic interest to it. I decided to place this fabric so that the second print was a small arc.

7. Then I sewed the black and white print to the pieced curve block, not worrying about matching ends. Remember, you are making an *oversized* block; you will have plenty of fabric to cut out your final 8½" square.

8. Now that I like the look of this block, I will square it up to 8½" x 8½" to make a Block A.

9. In Figure 9, the block is squared at 8½". Repeat the same process to make your remaining curved blocks. Refer to the cutting table for the sizes needed.

IMPORTANT TIP FOR MAKING CURVED BLOCKS: ONE AT A TIME

Work on one curved block at a time. When you are finished, place it on your design wall or table so that you can see it. Make sure you are varying the fabrics and solids used so that each block is interesting and unique.

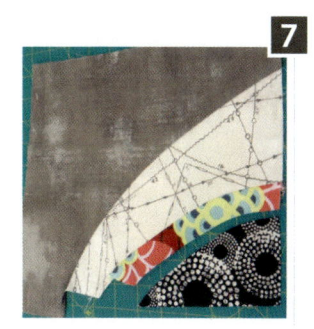

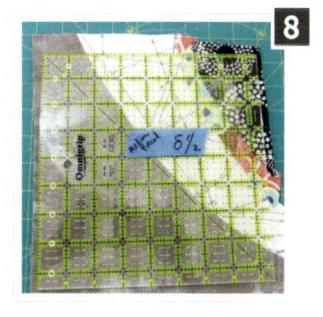

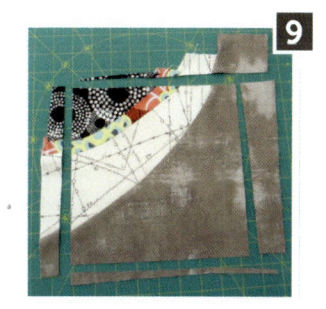

A NOTE ABOUT IMPROVISATION AND INCREASING QUILT SIZE

Remember that you have options for how you lay out the blocks in this quilt. *To make the quilt larger,* you can add more pieced and background blocks. You can also add asymmetrical borders using the instructions at the end of this project. *To get different looks,* you can move the A and B blocks around. You can change the format of a block. You can take a background block such as Block B and make it a pieced curve block. You can take a Block A and make it a background block.

MADLY MODERN QUILTS

CUTTING TABLE

BLOCK A 13 pieced curve blocks 8½" x 8½"	BLOCK B 10 blocks 8½" x 8½" Background fabric
BLOCK C: One block 2½" x 24½" Background fabric	BLOCK D: One block 3½" x 16½" Background fabric
BLOCK E: One block 3½" x 5½" Background fabric	BLOCK F: Two pieced curve blocks 5½" x 5½"
BLOCK G: One block 3½" x 8½" Background fabric	BLOCK H: Four blocks 2½" x 8½" Background fabric
BLOCK I: One block 5½" x 11½" Background fabric	BLOCK J: One pieced curve block 3½" x 5½"
BLOCK K: One block 3½" x 3½" Background fabric	BLOCK L: One block 5½" x 8½" Background fabric
BLOCK M: One block 3½" x 16½" Background fabric	

CUTTING THE BACKGROUND BLOCKS

Cut the number and sizes of background blocks from your background fabric according to the cutting table. These are blocks B, C, D, E, G, H, I, K, L and M.

MAKING THE QUILT LARGER BY ADDING BORDERS

You can easily make this quilt larger by adding four borders made from the background fabric. The center of the quilt remains the same as explained in the earlier sections of this project.

Here are the suggested border sizes to make a quilt measuring 54" x 66":

› *Top Border:* 4½" x 71½"
› *Left Border:* 8½" x 56½"
› *Right Border:* 12½" x 56½"
› *Bottom Border:* 6½" x 71½"

You will need an additional 1½ yards of your neutral fabric. (All other fabric requirements remain the same.)

FREEFORM TIPS: CHANGING YOUR LAYOUT

Changing the layout is easy!

You can change the quantity of Curved Block A's. For example, you might decide that you want only nine pieced curved blocks. In that case, you would make fourteen Block B's.

You can add solid 8½" squares (Block B). Perhaps you want to make five blocks out of the background fabric, and five out of solids or prints.

Blocks C, D, E, F, G and H can also be made from any combination of background fabric, solids and prints.

ASSEMBLY DIAGRAM

FINISHING AND BINDING

Assemble your quilt using the Assembly Diagram. Assemble your quilt top, batting and backing. Baste quilt.

I quilted my project with matchstick straight line stitching with my walking foot. I quilted curved lines by echoing the design in the curved blocks—also with my walking foot. I used a gray thread that blended into the background fabric. I also used a pale turquoise thread for some of the quilting to add variety to the surface.

After finishing the machine quilting, I added hand quilting using size 8 Perle cotton thread in coordinating colors. You can see the hand quilting in this close-up photo.

I made a faced binding for my project. Another interesting option is to make a pieced binding using the background fabric and print scraps.

FREEFORM TIPS: HAND QUILTING

Hand quilting with Size 8 Perle cotton (an embroidery thread) adds a bold graphic element to the curves. I often use some hand quilting to supplement my machine quilting. When I hand quilt, I use big stitches. I never mark the quilting line. In this case, it was more or less easy to follow the curve in the block! I chose thread colors that would show up against the curve, because bold contrast is an element of modern quilts.

MADLY MODERN QUILTS

5 DISAPPEARING FOUR PATCH #1

FINISHED SIZE: 54" x 71"

DISAPPEARING FOUR PATCH #1 QUILT

INTRODUCTION

This quilt is created using an altered version of a very traditional block—the Four Patch. The quilt is an example of modern traditionalism. A traditional Four Patch Block is made from four squares cut exactly the same size from print fabrics.

To make it more modern, I altered the dimensions of the Four Patch so that the patches are not four equal squares. I also used background fabric in the Four Patch blocks. Finally, I added a randomly pieced border.

You will have extra pieces of fabric after you piece the Four Patch Blocks, but don't worry! You can use the extras to create the pieced random border or in the binding as you can see in this example.

You will use these modern quilting design elements:
› Alternate grid layout
› Use of negative space
› Modern traditionalism

FREEFORM PATTERN TIP: IMPROVISE
There is an improvisational version of this quilt in the following chapter.

MATERIALS LIST

To make this quilt, you will need:
› 5/8 yard of a vibrant modern print *(floral in this sample)*
› *Solids:* Choose your solids by looking at the color dots on the selvedge of your print. I suggest buying ¼ yard as cut yardage, not a fat quarter. This will make cutting out your blocks easier.
    › ¼ yard of solid #1 *(green in this sample)*
    › ¼ yard of solid #2 *(blue in this sample)*
    › ¼ yard of solid #3 *(pink in this sample)*
    › ¼ yard of solid #4 *(yellow in this sample)*
    › ¼ yard of solid #5 *(orange in this sample)*
› 3⅞ yards of solid or near solid for your background fabric and binding *(white in this sample)*
› *Batting:* 58" x 75"
› *Backing:* 3¾ yards backing fabric

PATRIOTIC VERSION

To make this quilt in a patriotic palette, choose a bold modern print in red, white and blue (or your country's national colors) for your focus fabric and then choose coordinating solids and prints.

MADLY MODERN QUILTS

MAKING FOUR PATCH BLOCKS

The block is made with four patches and measures 9½" x 9½" unfinished.

Here are the *unfinished* sizes of each patch:

A: 3½" x 3½" square
B: 3½" x 6½" rectangle (*two* per block)
C: 6½" x 6½" square

CUTTING TABLE

Here are the instructions showing the number of squares and rectangles to cut to make the version shown in the project sample.

Fabric	3½" squares	3½" x 6½" rectangles	6½" squares
Focus Print Fabric	1	3	4
Solid #1 *(pink)*	0	4	1
Solid #2 *(yellow)*	3	1	0
Solid #3 *(blue)*	2	0	2
Solid #4 *(green)*	2	4	0
Solid #5 *(orange)*	3	1	1
Background Fabric *(white)*	2	13	5

FREEFORM TIP: MAKE IT YOUR OWN

You can easily make this quilt your own by changing the number of fabric colors, such as using just three solids or using a bold geometric print instead of one of the solids. You can also change it up by cutting more of a color that you want to feature and reducing the number of squares or rectangles for another color. For example, instead of cutting four 3½" x 6½" rectangles in Solid #1, you could cut only two of them and substitute two of another color (such as Solid #2).

FREEFORM TIP: SHOW OFF

Use this quilt to show off your favorite designer prints. You only need small quantities, so you could use leftovers from another project.

ASSEMBLY INSTRUCTIONS

Four Patch Blocks

Assemble thirteen pieced blocks from the squares and rectangles. Sew A to B. Sew B to C. Sew the two resulting pieces together. Your pieced Four Patch block will measure 9½" x 9½".

Background Blocks

Cut seventeen 9½" x 9½" squares from your background fabric.

Pieced Improvisational Border E

This border (E) measures 5½" x 46½". Using leftover pieces of the print, solid and background fabric, randomly piece sections together until you have a strip that measures 47½" x 5½". This is where you can have some improvisational fun.

Borders A, B, C, D, F

Long borders can be pieced from background fabric. From your background fabric, make the following:

> Borders A and C: 5½ x 71½"
> Border B: 5½ x 46½"
> Border D: 3½ x 46½"
> Border F: 4½ x 46½"

DISAPPEARING FOUR PATCH #1 QUILT

ASSEMBLY DIAGRAM

When you assemble the quilt top, you can turn the pieced Four Patch blocks in different directions to get an improvisational look.

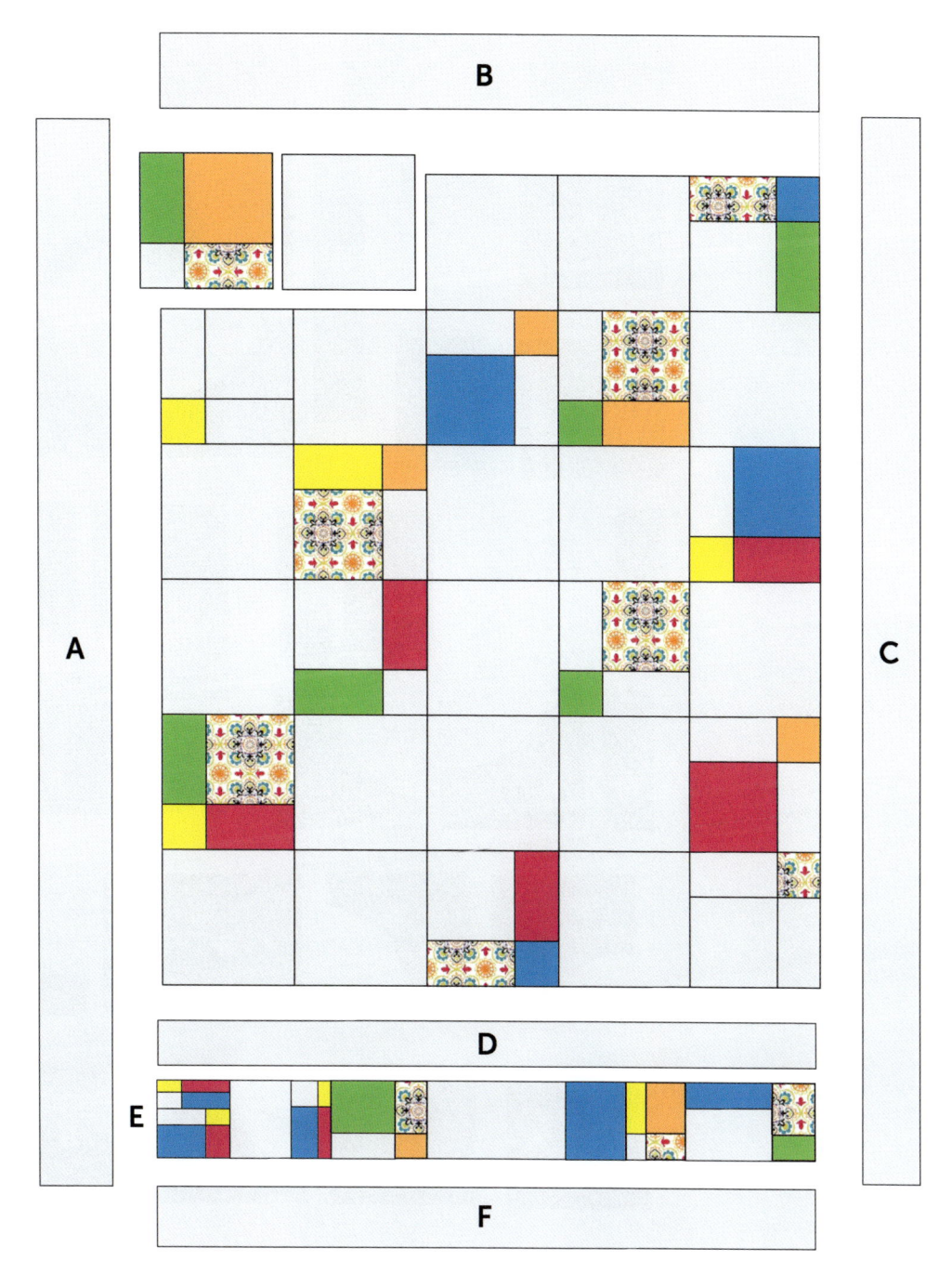

FINISHING AND BINDING

Assemble your quilt using the Assembly Diagram.

Layer the quilt top, batting and backing. Baste and quilt as desired. A modern floral quilting motif would be fun for this quilt if you use a bold floral as your focus fabric. I recommend using a thread color that blends into your background fabric.

For the binding in the example, I randomly pieced leftover prints and solids with background fabric.

MADLY MODERN QUILTS

43

6 DISAPPEARING THREE PATCH / FOUR PATCH QUILT

FINISHED SIZE: 56" x 56"

44 DISAPPEARING THREE PATCH / FOUR PATCH QUILT

INTRODUCTION

For this version, I created a different layout. The grid from the Disappearing Four Patch Quilt on p. 40 has been altered to create a more improvisational look. I call this Three Patch / Four Patch because I've added a new pieced Three Patch Block that mimics the Four Patch Block. You can easily adapt this pattern further to create your own unique layout.

You will use these modern quilting design elements:

› asymmetry
› use of negative space
› alternate grid layout

Materials estimates are generous so that you can modify how you place each color in the blocks and arrange the negative space for the layout. Leftovers can be used to piece an improvisational quilt back and can be used in the binding.

FREEFORM TIP: SHOW OFF

Use this quilt to show off your favorite designer print. You only need small quantities so you could use up leftovers from another project.

MATERIALS LIST

Fabric you will need:

› ⅜ yard of a vibrant large scale modern print *(floral in this sample)*
› *Solids:* Choose your solids by looking at the color dots on the selvedge of your print. I suggest buying ¼ yard as cut yardage, not a fat quarter. This will make cutting out your blocks easier.
  › ⅛ yard of solid #1 *(light green in this sample)*
  › ¼ yard of solid #2 *(dark green in this sample)*
  › ¼ yard of solid #3 *(orange in this sample)*
  › ¼ yard of solid #4 *(purple in this sample)*
  › ¼ yard of solid #5 *(yellow in this sample)*
  › ¼ yard of solid #6 *(dotted print in this sample)*
› 3½ yards of solid or near solid for your background fabric and binding *(gray in this sample)*
› *Batting:* 59" x 59"
› *Backing:* 3¾ yards backing fabric

MADLY MODERN QUILTS

CUTTING TABLE: PIECED BLOCKS

The Four Patch block is made from four Patches and measures 9½" x 9½" unfinished. Here are the *unfinished* sizes of each patch in the Four Patch version:

› *A:* 3½" x 3½" square
› *B:* 3½" x 6½" rectangles (*two* per block)
› *C:* 6½" x 6½" square

The three patch block is made from three patches and measures 9½" x 9½" unfinished. This is a *new* version of the block where you will use a 3½" x 9½" patch. The block becomes a three patch that mimics the four patch and adds to the improvisational effect.

Fabric	Number and size of patches to cut
Print Fabric	Five 3½" x 6½" rectangles
	Three 6½" x 6½" squares
Solid #1 (*light green*)	One 3½" x 3½" square
	Four 3½" x 6½" rectangles
	One 6½" x 6½" square
Solid #2 (*dark green*)	One 3½" x 6½" rectangle
	One 6½" x 6½" square
Solid #3 (*orange*)	One 3½" x 3½" square
	One 3½" x 6½" rectangles
	Two 6½" x 6½" squares
	One 3½" x 9½" rectangle
Solid #4 (*purple*)	Five 3½" x 3½" squares
	One 3½" x 9½" rectangle
Solid #5 (*yellow*)	Two 3½" x 3½" squares
	Four 3½" x 6½" rectangles
	Two 6½" x 6½" squares
Solid #6 (*dotted print*)	One 3½" x 3½" square
	Two 3½ x 6½" rectangles
	Two 6½" x 6½" squares
Background Fabric	Four 3½ x 6½" rectangles
	One 6½" x 6½" square

INSTRUCTIONS FOR MAKING PIECED BLOCKS

Assemble fourteen pieced blocks from the squares and rectangles. But this time, instead of following the same layout, you can mix it up like in the examples shown here.

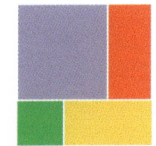

The four patches are arranged in different positions.

This is the Three Patch block made with one 6½" x 6½" square; one 3½" x 6½" rectangle and one 3½" x 9½" rectangle.

FREEFORM TIP: BIGGER OR SMALLER

Make this quilt bigger by adding asymmetrical borders to the top, right and bottom, and widening Block A. Or you can *make this quilt smaller* by eliminating the first column of blocks that includes Blocks B, C, D and the two Four Patch blocks.

FINISHING AND BINDING

Assemble your quilt using the Assembly Diagram.

Layering, basting and quilting: Layer the quilt top, backing and batting. Then baste and quilt as desired. I recommend straight line quilting using a thread color that blends into your background fabric. I also suggest adding occasional lines of quilting using a contrasting color (variegated, bold or subtle—it's your choice!)

Binding: Create a binding using leftover background fabric with randomly sized sections of the other fabrics. This is improvisational, so the choice of fabric and placement is up to you.

FREEFORM TIP: BREAK IT UP

Notice that Blocks E, F, G and H are actually a four patch broken into parts. You can break up other four patch blocks the same way and have fun with the layout without any additional measuring.

DISAPPEARING 3 PATCH / 4 PATCH QUILT

CUTTING TABLE: BLOCKS A-T

Cut the following from your background fabric—longer sections will be pieced.

A: 4½" x 56½"	B: 9½" x 13½"	C: 9½" x 20½"	D: 9½" x 5½"	E: 6½" x 6½"	I: 9½" x 3½"
J: 9½" x 17½"	K: 7½" x 35½"	L: 34½" x 12½"	M: 14½" x 9½"	N: 9½" x 13½"	O: 9½" x 4½"
P: 9½" x 9½"	Q: 9½" x 8½"	R: 9½" x 3½"	S: 9½" x 14½"	T: 11½" x 9½"	

Cut the following from solid colors.

F: 3½" x 6½" (Solid #3—orange)	G: 6½" x 3½" (Solid #1—light green)	H: 3½" x 3½" (Solid #4—purple)

ASSEMBLY DIAGRAM

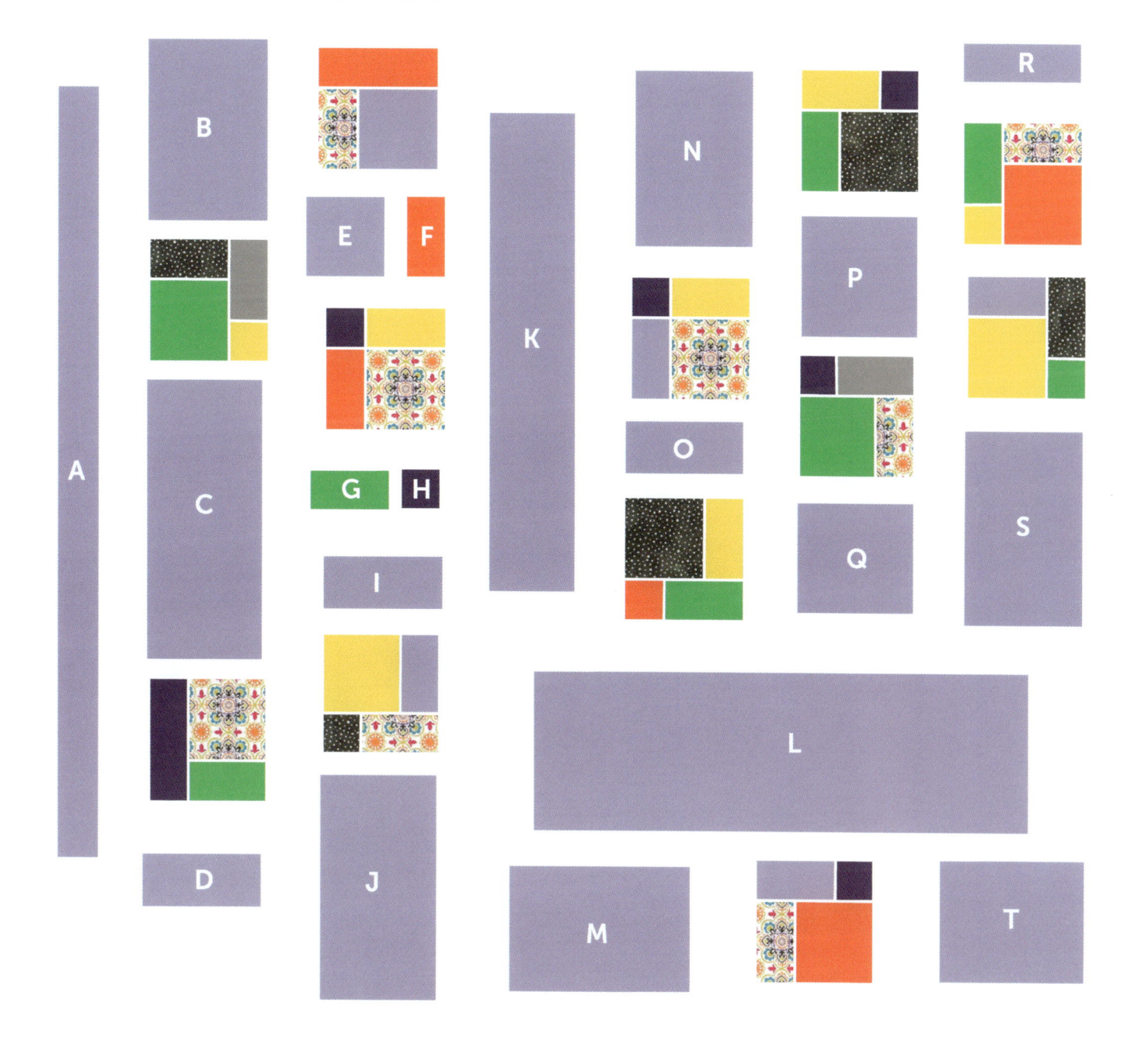

MADLY MODERN QUILTS

7 MARSALA IMPROV #1 QUILT

FINISHED SIZE: 53" x 60"

MARSALA IMPROV #1 QUILT

INTRODUCTION

I designed this quilt in response to an online challenge to make a quilt using the Pantone color of the year, Marsala, which is a wine or burgundy color. There weren't a lot of fabric choices in the shops at the time because it is an unusual color. I decided to "shop my stash" to create this quilt.

Fortunately, I quickly found a bold modern print in my stash that had Marsala flowers and several other interesting colors. In fact, this fabric had been sitting in my stash for a long time because it was so bold that it never seemed to work with other prints. This fabric became my focus fabric.

Since this was a modern quilt, I wanted to create a lot of negative space. I noticed that the focus print had quite a bit of white in it, so I used a white tone-on-tone as my background fabric, but I could also have chosen a lighter tint of one of the solids. After testing some other colors, I decided that I liked the bold contrast achieved by using white as my background fabric.

Next, I found a solid fabric that was a close approximation of Marsala. The challenge requirement was to use "a lot" of the Marsala color in the quilt. I'm not sure I fulfilled that requirement, because I didn't want a dark quilt and I decided to use more bright colors and white.

That led me to another idea: to use solids for the other colors in the quilt. It's very easy to figure out which solid colors to use. Look for the color dots printed on the selvedge; this will always help you select solids (or even other prints) that will work with your focus fabric. Then, you can choose darker or lighter versions of those colors. I went bold with the solids and added a lime green to the selection for more spark. I added black and white prints for more contrast and sparkle.

This project will give you an opportunity to make a lot of improvisationally pieced squares. There is no pattern or template for the improvisational blocks. Instead, I've provided a few tips for randomly piecing these fun squares. By the time you finish this project, you'll be a pro at improvisational piecing.

You will use these modern quilting design elements:
› Alternate grid layout
› Use of negative space
› Modern traditionalism
› Improvisation

MATERIALS LIST

Fabric you will need for the quilt top and binding:
› 4 yards --background fabric *(white tone-on-tone in sample)*
› One Fat quarter of a bold modern print *(focus fabric)*
› Large scraps or fat eighths of at least six different solids—colors that complement the focus fabric. In the sample quilt, I used marsala (burgundy), yellow, black, dark green, lime green, light blue and dark blue.
› *Optional:* ⅛ yard or large scrap of a second print that complements and contrasts with the focus fabric. This might be a stripe or print that has a different scale.
› *Optional:* ⅛ yard or large scraps of one or two black and white prints. I chose to use black and white prints because they complemented my focus fabric (it had white and black in it) and because I liked the way they contrasted with the white tone-on-tone background fabric.
› *Batting:* at least 58" x 65"
› *Backing fabric:* 3¾ yards

My focus fabric: This project can be a great stash buster! Use up some of those beautiful scraps.

MADLY MODERN QUILTS

PLANNING THIS IMPROVISATIONAL QUILT

This quilt has eleven rows of squares. I didn't plan these rows in advance, although I had a general idea that I wanted the quilt to measure at least 50" square. I started with an idea that I wanted to use 3½" squares cut from each of the fabrics and lay them out in rows. However, after cutting out about 40 of these squares, I decided that I needed to add more visual interest. I then added two more types of squares: half-square triangles and improvisationally pieced squares.

I then started making half-square triangle squares and improvisationally pieced squares. I made these squares and rearranged them in rows with the original squares on my design wall until I was satisfied with the overall design. Of course, I had a few blocks left over that I did not use in the quilt.

I encourage you to take this same approach—planning and piecing as you go—to create your own unique layout. Experiment and have fun. Make a few blocks at a time and arrange them on your design wall. Don't sew the rows together until you are satisfied with your overall layout. (If you don't have space for a permanent design wall, see my tip about making a portable wall in the first chapter of the book.)

Fabrics used in this quilt

I suggest you take frequent in-progress photos of your layout on your design wall. Check for color placement and use of negative space.

To make a quilt the size shown in the sample, you will need a total of 132 squares. Each row has twelve squares in it. Each row has three types of squares:
1. squares cut from fabric (no piecing)
2. improvisationally pieced squares
3. half square triangles (HSTs)

The cutting table will give you detail on how many squares of each type are in this quilt. Remember—you can use any combination that you like! One version is shown in the photo of the sample quilt. In the assembly diagram on p. 55, I've used this same combination of squares in a different layout. The possibilities are endless!

Notice that there are places in the quilt where there are white background fabric squares next to each other. I decided to sew these white 3½" squares together to maintain the underlying grid structure in the quilt.

MARSALA IMPROV #1 QUILT

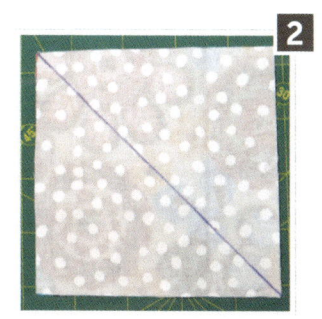

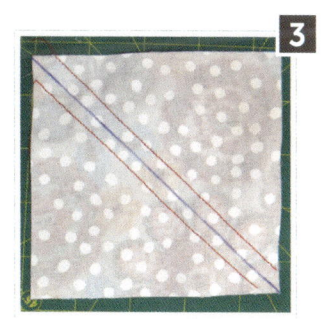

MAKING HALF-SQUARE TRIANGLES (HSTs)

There are many methods for making half-square triangle units (HSTs). Instead of using templates, try this fast and easy method. You can find tutorials for this method and other methods online.

Make a test HST following these instructions BEFORE cutting up all of your fabric!

1. Cut two 4" squares from two different fabrics.

2. Place the fabric right sides together. Draw a diagonal line from one corner to the other. I use a regular number 2 pencil and draw very lightly. (In the image above, I used a blue pen so you can see my drawn line.)

3. Stitch on both sides of your drawn line using a ¼" seam. (I used red thread in this example so you can see my two stitch lines.)

4. Cut the square in half on the drawn line.

5. Press open with seam allowances going towards the darker fabric. Press very lightly so the units don't stretch. Sometimes I give these triangle units a light spray of starch or Best Press™ to keep them stable.

6. Trim the open squares to 3½". Use a square ruler to trim. You will have very little waste. And, you'll save a lot of time because you will be making two at a time! When I have to make several half-square triangles, I use blue tape to mark off the size on my ruler. On this ruler, there is a diagonal line that I lay directly on the seam to help me keep my HSTs even.

7. Trimmed 3½" block and small leftovers. This method has a tiny bit of waste, but it's worth it to get accurate HSTs. Sometimes I use these leftovers in my improvisationally pieced squares.

8. PROBLEMS? If your HST is too small, then your 1/4" seam allowance may be off. An easy fix is to start step #1 with two 4-1/4" or 4-1/2" squares. Experiment to see what works best for you.

MADLY MODERN QUILTS

MAKING IMPROVISATIONAL SQUARES

This is the step where you get to just let go and sew! No planning and no measuring needed.

When I make improvisational pieced blocks, I start by sewing small pieces of fabric together into what I call "sets". The sets can be any size or shape. I make different sets and then start to combine them. I sew fabrics together randomly until I have a "square-ish" unit measuring about 4½" or more on each side. These sets do *not* have regular edges. Then, I cut my 3½" square from the most interesting part of this improvisational block. I save the leftovers to use in another block.

Sometimes I'll make improvisational blocks that are much larger so that I can cut two blocks from them. For example, I might make an improvisational block measuring 8" square (more or less). Then I cut two 3½" squares from this larger unit. After trimming, I keep the leftovers and use them in the next improvisational block.

Use your own ideas to make variations. For example, in this quilt, I sewed black 1" strips to solid color rectangles to make an improvisational striped block. I liked the resulting small strip of black. In the blocks, the finished size of the black strip is ½". You could make yours even narrower.

When you are making improvisationally pieced blocks, keep rotating the piece you are working on and continue sewing on new sections. You are *not* making a log cabin—make sure the block doesn't get too regular. Avoid making cuts that are parallel, so you avoid sections that line up too much. Too many parallel lines will make your block boring. Make some of your cuts at an angle. I use rulers to keep the cuts straight but I am *not* measuring anything until the end of the process. Don't overthink the process. Grab a section, sew it on, grab another piece of fabric, sew it on... and so forth. See p. 76 for an improvisational process.

I pieced a 4" freehand curve block using the marsala (burgundy) and white fabric. (See Parisian Curves Quilt for more examples of how to make improvisationally pieced curve blocks.) I then randomly cut this curve block into sections and used the pieces in other improvisational blocks.

Close up of an improvisationally pieced block (showing white and yellow thread used for quilting). I quilted this project using different colors of thread—white, yellow and blue. I quilted it with randomly spaced straight lines on my home machine using my walking foot.

MARSALA IMPROV #1 QUILT

An in-progress shot on my design wall. I play as I go, placing the squares on the wall as I make them.

Close-up: rows in progress.

After piecing the rows, I decided the quilt needed more negative space between the groups of rows. I grouped the rows into four sets: a single row at the top; a set of two rows; a set of five rows and a bottom set of three rows.

I added strips made from the white fabric between the sets (See rows A, B, C in the Assembly Diagram).

MADLY MODERN QUILTS

53

CUTTING TABLE

To make this quilt, here's how many of each type of square you will need. Notice that the squares in the Assembly Diagram are arranged differently from the sample quilt pictured at the beginning of this project. I wanted to show you how easily you can vary your quilt. You can make the same number of squares shown in this table and rearrange them in any way that you like! Remember, you can change the quantities you make of each square for even more variety. Do make sure you have enough background fabric squares to create a good amount of negative space.

Type of Square 3½" x 3½"	Number included in sample layout	Number you will include in your layout
Background fabric	46	
Focus Print	5	
Solid #1 (yellow)	4	
Solid #2 (Marsala - dark burgundy)	8	
Solid #3 (blue)	6	
Solid #4 (green)	3	
Solid #5 (black)	1	
Half-Square Triangle squares (HSTs)	26	
Improvisationally pieced squares (see instructions)	23	
Black and white prints	10	
Total squares needed	132	

MAKING BORDERS

Cut the following borders from your background fabric. You will have to piece the longer sections:

› A: 2½" x 36½"
› B: 4½" x 36½"
› C: 5½" x 36½"
› D: 5½" x 53½"
› E: 8½" x 44½"
› F: 11½" x 53½"
› G: 9½" x 44½"

> **FREEFORM TIP: BOLD BORDERS**
> You can add additional improvisationally pieced squares into the borders.

FINISHING AND BINDING

Assemble your quilt using the Assembly Diagram.

Layering, basting and quilting: Layer the quilt top, backing and batting. Then baste and quilt as desired. I recommend straight line quilting using a thread color that blends into your background fabric. I also suggest adding occasional lines of quilting using a contrasting color (variegated, bold or subtle—it's your choice!)

Binding: Create a binding using leftover background fabric with randomly sized sections of the other fabrics. This is improvisational, so the choice of fabric and placement is up to you.

ASSEMBLY DIAGRAM

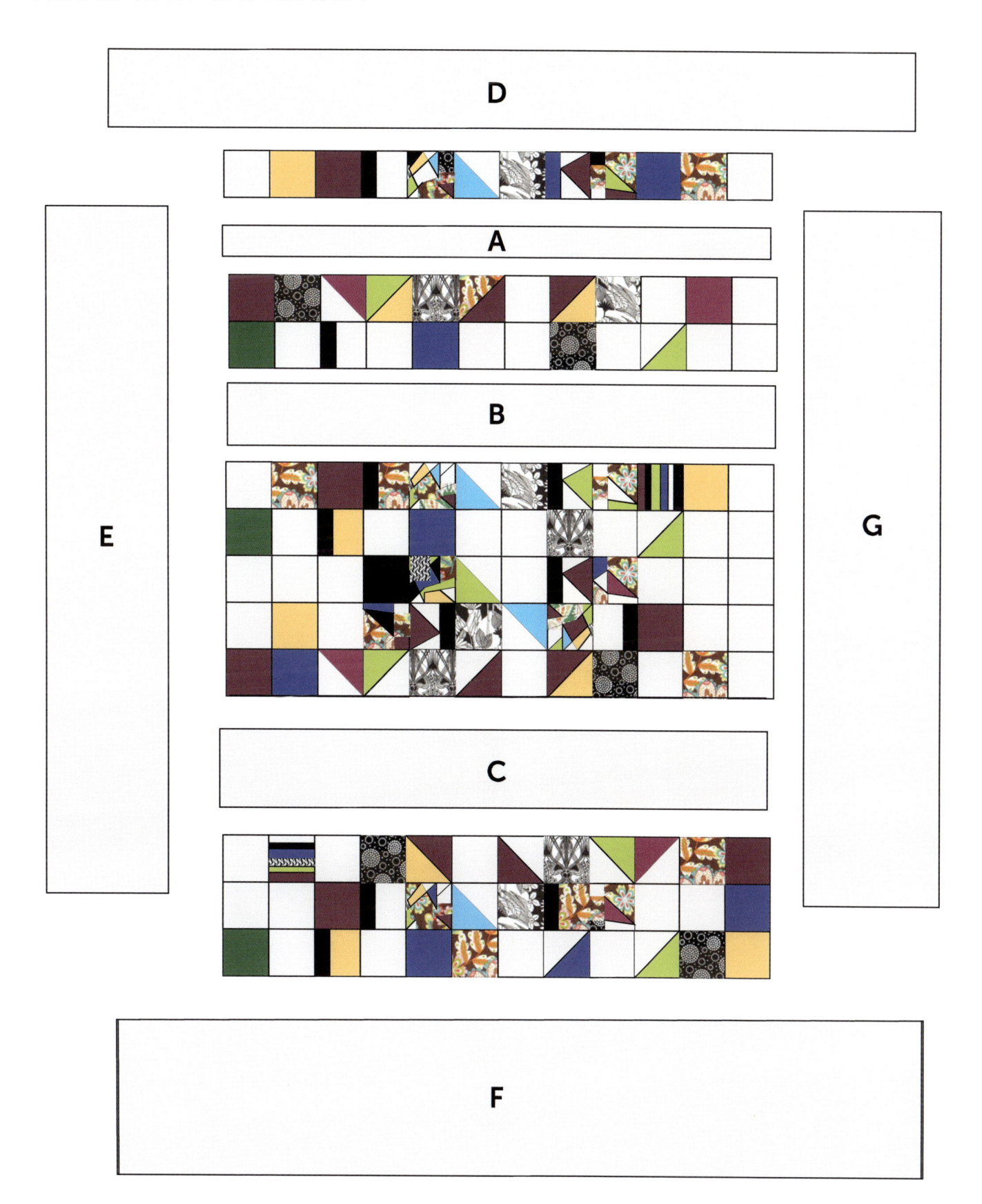

MADLY MODERN QUILTS

8 DISAPPEARING NINE PATCH WITH IMPROV BLOCKS

FINISHED SIZE: 55" x 55"

FREEFORM TIP: MAKE YOUR QUILT LARGER
If you want to make this quilt larger, you can add one or more columns with a Nine Patch block in them, or you can add asymmetrical borders on one or more sides, top or bottom.

DISAPPEARING NINE PATCH WITH IMPROV BLOCKS

INTRODUCTION

This is a very simple quilt that can have dramatic effect. It is a great project if you want to practice free motion quilting because it has a lot of negative space.

You will use these modern quilting design elements:

› improvisation
› use of negative space
› alternate grid layout
› reinterpretation of the past.

MATERIALS LIST

To create the sample, I first decided on a yellow, white and gray color scheme. I chose white for my background fabric to create negative space. Then, I searched through my scrap bin for fabrics that would work and used them to create the solid blocks and the improvisational blocks.

To make a quilt that is 55" x 55", you will need:

› 3 yards-- background solid *(white in sample)*
› ¼ yard stripe fabric
› ¼ yard solid #1 *(gray in sample)*
› ¼ yard solid #2 *(yellow in sample)*
› Assorted print scraps for improvisational blocks
› Small scraps of one to three solid colors for improvisational blocks *(deep gold, purple and red in sample)*
› Batting: 59" x 59"
› Backing: 3¾ yards

MAKING NINE PATCH BLOCKS

For this project, I created three Nine Patch Blocks that measure 15½" x 15½". You will need a total of 27 squares, each measuring 5½" unfinished. This chart shows what I used to make my quilt. I've left a blank column for you to make notes if you decide to modify the quilt to suit your own style. If you decide to change the number of each type of square, be sure to include at least two background squares in each Nine Patch Block to bring the negative space into the Nine Patch Blocks.

CUTTING TABLE: SQUARES

Type of Square 5½" x 5½"	Number included in sample layout	Number you will include in your layout
Background fabric *(white)*	10	
Stripe Fabric	2	
Solid #1 *(gray in sample)*	6	
Solid #2 *(yellow in sample)*	3	
Improvisationally pieced squares	6	

MADLY MODERN QUILTS

MAKING IMPROVISATIONAL BLOCKS

Follow the instructions in the Marsala Improv Quilt and the Fractured Disappearing Nine Patch for additional examples of improvisationally pieced blocks. For this project, I used a deep gold, red and purple fabric to give the improvisational blocks a *pop* of color. Here are some examples showing my process for the sample quilt.

1. First, I chose fabrics from my stash (Figure 1). I happened to have fat quarters and half-yards, but you could use large scraps instead. After laying out the fabric, I decided that the improvisational blocks needed some accent colors for *pop*.

2. I like to audition selections before doing any cutting and piecing. I auditioned a bright purple [left Figure 2] and liked the way it brought out the yellows. When I auditioned a deep red, I thought it was exciting as well (right Figure 2).

3. When I make improvisationally pieced blocks, I piece the fabrics in sets and then cut and combine them. Here you see two of the sets I made. I pieced different fabrics in each set. I might repeat a fabric or two in a set but my goal is to make the sets look different. Each set measures about 4" on each side, although some might be larger.

4. Here you can see how I started combining sets together to make a larger block. I oversized the blocks; in this case I made the blocks at least 6" long and wide—or larger. Then I chose the most interesting section to cut out as my 5½" square.

When you are making improvisationally pieced blocks, keep rotating the piece you are working on and continue sewing on new sections. You are not making a log cabin—make sure the block doesn't get too regular.

Avoid making cuts that are parallel. Make some of your cuts at an angle. I use rulers to keep the cuts straight, but I don't measure until I'm ready to cut out my final 5½" square. Don't overthink the process. Grab a section, sew it on, grab another piece of fabric, sew it on...and so forth! *See p.76 for another fun way to make improvisationally pieced blocks.*

DISAPPEARING NINE PATCH WITH IMPROV BLOCKS

ASSEMBLY DIAGRAM

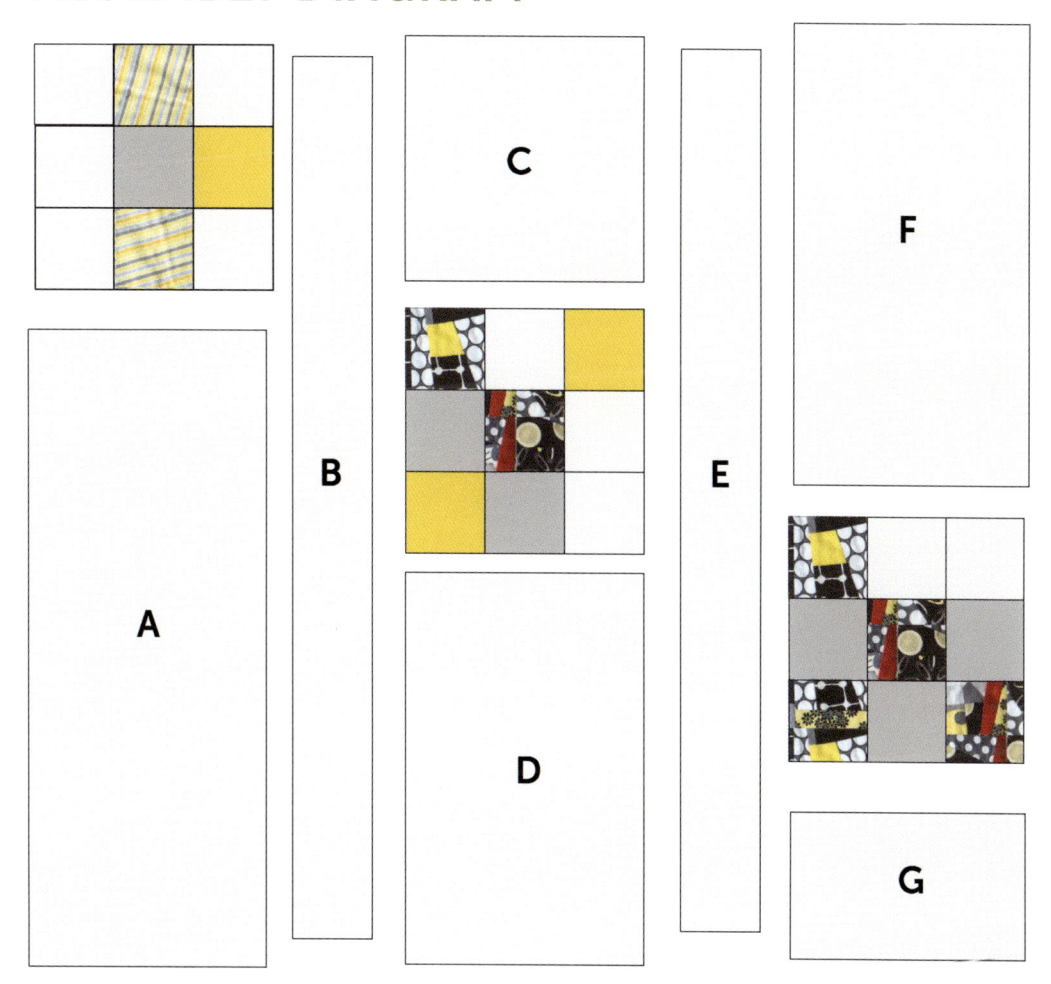

CUTTING TABLE: BACKGROUND FABRIC

Here are the unfinished sizes for the background sections. You will have to piece the longer sections:

- › *A:* 15½" x 40½"
- › *B:* 5½" x 55½"
- › *C:* 15½" x 15½"
- › *D:* 15½" x 25½"
- › *E:* 5½" x 55½"
- › *F:* 15½" x 30½"
- › *G:* 15½" x 10½"

FINISHING AND BINDING

Assemble your quilt using the Assembly Diagram.

Layering, basting and quilting: Layer the quilt top, backing and batting. Then baste and quilt as desired. Because of all the negative space, this quilt is a great opportunity to try free motion quilting on your domestic or long-arm machine. Or, you can quilt matchstick straight line quilting or other modern motifs with your walking foot. I recommend using a thread color that blends into your background fabric. I also suggest adding occasional lines of quilting using a contrasting color (variegated, bold or subtle—it's your choice!)

Binding: Create a binding using leftover background fabric with randomly sized sections of the other fabrics. This is improvisational, so the choice of fabric and placement is up to you. The use of randomly spaced print or solid fabrics helps to frame the negative space.

MADLY MODERN QUILTS

9 SPRING GARDEN DISAPPEARING NINE PATCH QUILT

FINISHED SIZES:
WALL HANGING: 22" x 35"
LAP QUILT: 64" x 73"

SPRING GARDEN DISAPPEARING NINE PATCH QUILT

INTRODUCTION

These instructions include options for making two quilts from improvisationally laid out Nine Patch Blocks. In this sample, I've used a fresh spring palette of solids and prints. You can make this quilt using a combination of larger scraps or leftover yardage. The lap quilt size is a great project for using your favorite modern designer fabrics because the blocks let the designs and colors really show off.

You will use these modern quilting design elements:
› Alternate grid layout
› Use of negative space
› Modern traditionalism

MATERIALS LIST: WALL HANGING

› 1 yard of a solid or tone-on-tone background fabric
› 1/8 yard or scraps of at least seven different fabrics in your chosen palette or from a favorite designer. Scraps need to be at least 2½" square.
› *Batting:* 26" x 39"
› *Backing:* 26" x 39"

MATERIALS LIST: LAP QUILT

› 4⅛ yards of a solid or tone-on-tone background fabric
› 1/8 yard or large scraps of at least ten different fabrics in your chosen palette or from a favorite designer. Scraps must be at least 3½" x 3½".
› *Batting:* 68" x 77"
› *Backing:* 4½ yards

MADLY MODERN QUILTS

NINE PATCH BLOCK INSTRUCTIONS

The piecing is very simple for this quilt. The cutting tables show how many squares you need.

The fun begins as you make each Nine Patch Block. Each Nine Patch will include three or more background fabric squares and a variety of the other fabrics. Mix up the layouts so that no two Nine Patch Blocks are alike. The assembly diagrams give you some ideas. Mix it up using your imagination if you like! A design wall comes in handy so that you can easily see how each Nine Patch Block is different from the others.

CUTTING TABLE: WALL HANGING

Total Nine Patch Blocks: 9

Unfinished size of Nine Patch Block: 6½" x 6½"

Fabric	Number of 2½" squares needed
Assorted prints and colors	32
Background Fabric	49
Total 2½" squares needed	81

CUTTING TABLE: LAP QUILT

Total Nine Patch Blocks: 14

Unfinished size of Nine Patch Block: 9½" x 9½"

Fabric	Number of 3½" squares need
Assorted prints and colors	54
Background Fabric	72
Total 3½" squares needed	126

BACKGROUND BLOCKS

For the Wall Hanging, cut six squares measuring 6½" x 6½" from the background fabric.

For the Lap Quilt, cut twenty eight squares measuring 9½" x 9½" from the background fabric.

BORDERS

Wall Hanging

Cut borders from the background fabric:

› *A:* 2½" x 22½"
› *B and D:* 2½" x 30½"
› *C:* 3½" x 22½"

Lap Quilt

Piece borders from the background fabric:

› *A and C:* 5½" x 64½"
› *B and D:* 5½" x 63½

MORE RESOURCES ONLINE

Visit www.CaroleLylesShaw.com/MyBooks. Go to Additional Resources page for a blank planning sheet.

ASSEMBLY DIAGRAM: WALL HANGING

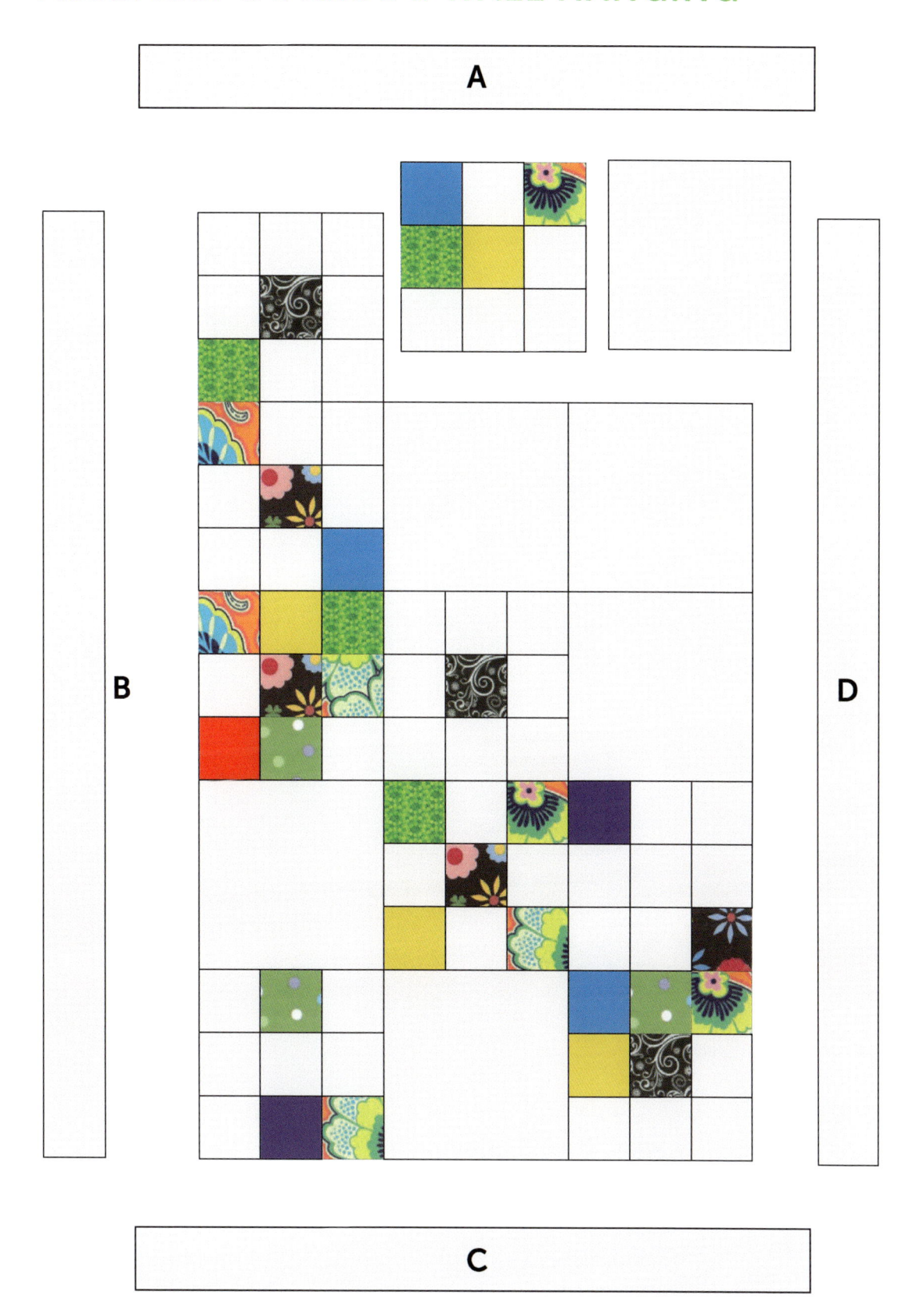

MADLY MODERN QUILTS

ASSEMBLY DIAGRAM: LAP QUILT

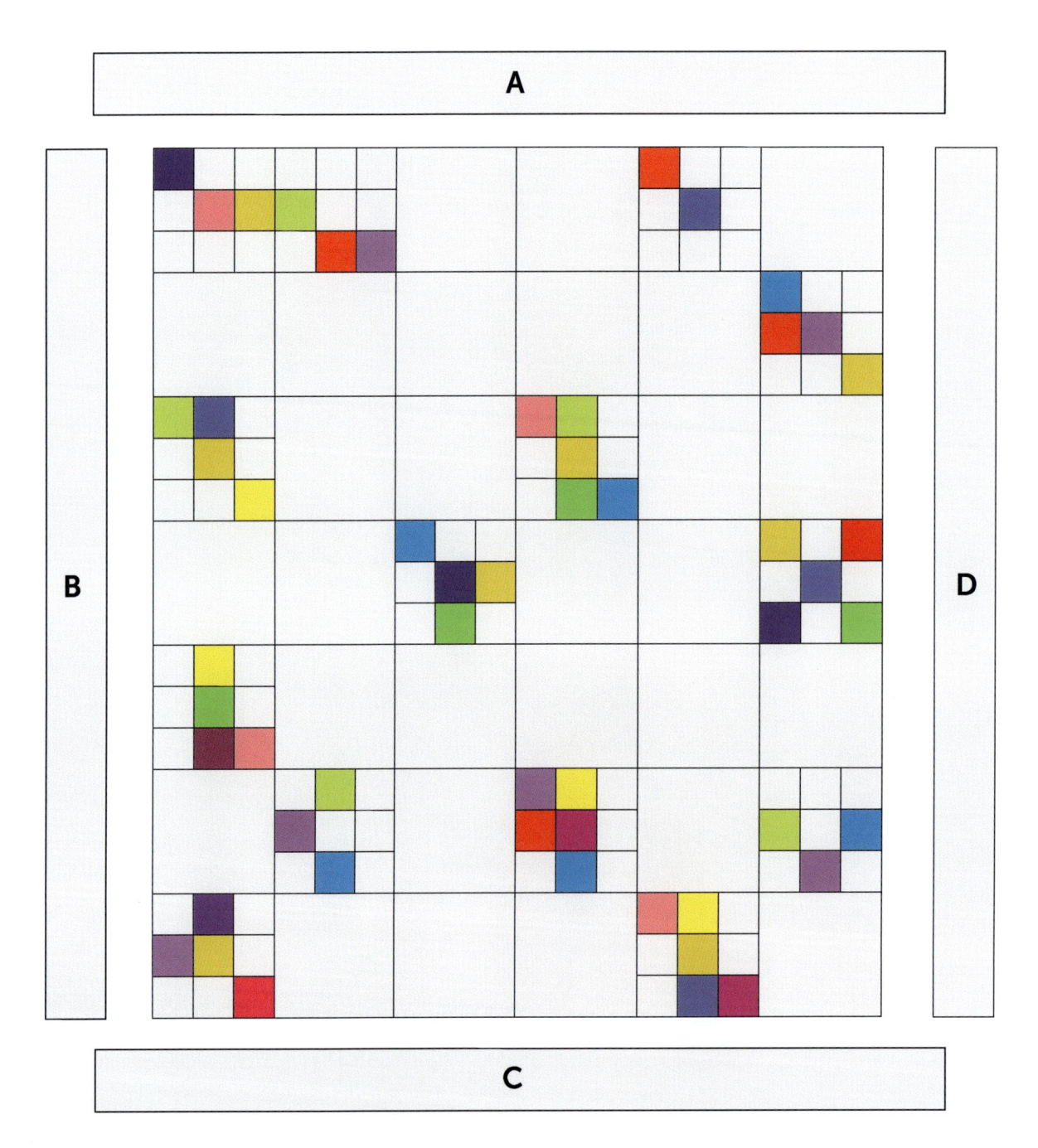

A

B

D

C

FINISHING AND BINDING

Assemble your quilt using the Assembly Diagram.

Layering, basting and quilting: Layer the quilt top, backing and batting. Then baste and quilt as desired. I recommend straight line quilting using a thread color that blends into your background fabric. I also suggest adding occasional lines of quilting using a contrasting color (variegated, bold or subtle—it's your choice!)

Binding: Create a binding using leftover background fabric with randomly sized sections of the other fabrics. This is improvisational, so the choice of fabric and placement is up to you.

SPRING GARDEN DISAPPEARING NINE PATCH QUILT

PLANNING YOUR QUILT

Ready to start planning your own quilt? Copy the template on this page. Use colored pencils or cut small pieces of fabric and glue them down to see how the colors might work.

MADLY MODERN QUILTS

10 LAYER CAKES AND RAIL FENCE IMPROV QUILT

FINISHED SIZES: 48" x 53" AND 58" x 68"

LAYER CAKES AND RAIL FENCE IMPROV QUILT

INTRODUCTION

This quilt is a stash buster and a great project for improvisational piecing. We all have wonderful layer cake blocks left over from other projects, as well as strips from jelly rolls we didn't quite use up in other projects. This project will help you use some of them up in a quilt that is a breeze to piece.

There are four blocks in this project:

› *Layer Cake Blocks:* whole squares that measure 9½" (finished size)
› *Rail Fence Blocks:* blocks pieced improvisationally that measure 9½" (finished size)
› *Half Size Blocks:* blocks pieced improvisationally that measure 9½" x 4¾" (finished size)
› *Border Blocks:* improvisationally pieced blocks that measure 4" (finished size)

Use a mix of solids and a few prints in the rail fence and border blocks in colors that coordinate with your large blocks.

You will use these modern quilting design elements:

› Alternate Grid layouts
› Improvisation
› Modern Traditionalism

MATERIALS LIST: 48" x 53" QUILT

To make the 48" x 53" quilt top, you will need:

› *Large Sqaure Focus Print(s):* approximately 1¼ yards total. You can use large scraps, fat quarters or 10" layer cake blocks in coordinating modern prints. *Solid or other neutral fabric* for borders and long sashing: 1½ yards
› *For Rail Fence Blocks:* A generous number of solids and prints from your stash
   › Scraps that measure at least 10" x 1" or 1½" wide
   › Jelly roll strips that you can cut into narrow strips measuring approximately 10" x 1" and 10" x 1½"
› *For Improv Pieced Blocks:* scraps left from making rail fence blocks

MATERIALS LIST: 58" x 68" QUILT

To make the 58" x 68" quilt top, you will need:

› *Large Square Focus Print(s):* approximately 1¾ yards total. You can use large scraps, fat quarters or 10" layer cake blocks in coordinating modern prints. *Solid or other neutral fabric* for borders and long sashing: 2½ yards
› *For Rail Fence Blocks:* A generous number of solids and prints from your stash
   › Scraps that measure at least 10" x 1" or 1½"
   › Jelly roll strips that you can cut into narrow strips measuring approximately 10" x 1" and 10" x 1½"
› *For Improv Pieced Blocks:* scraps left from making rail fence blocks

What do I mean by *"a generous number"*? With an improvisational project like this one, it is very hard to estimate. Start by going through your stash, selecting a pile of coordinating fabric and then dive into making the rail fence and border blocks. Here are some tips that might help:

› *Rail Fence Blocks:* Each block uses approximately 6 to 8 strips, with each strip measuring 10" in length. Go to your stash and find scraps that you can use to make 10" long strips. Each strip measures 1" wide or 1½" wide. Mix up the colors and prints for variety.
› *Improv Pieced Blocks:* Here you can use smaller scraps to make these improv blocks. You can also use leftover strips from the rail fence blocks as you can see in the detail photo.

MADLY MODERN QUILTS

PIECING INSTRUCTIONS

Use the Cutting Tables to cut and piece the blocks.

CUTTING TABLE: 48" x 53" QUILT

These are unfinished block sizes. Note that some sizes do not need the 1/2"!

Block	Fabric(s)	Size (")	Number
A	Layer Cake squares or various focus prints	10" x 10"	8
B	Pieced rail fence blocks - *Various prints and solids*	10" x 10"	8
C	Improvisationally pieced blocks *Various prints and solids*	3½" x 4½"	24
D	Border Block *Background fabric*	2½" x 48½"	2
E	Border Block *Background fabric*	2½" x 48½"	1
F	Border Block *Background fabric*	3½" x 38½"	3
G	Border Block *Background fabric*	4½" x 48½"	1

CUTTING TABLE: 58" x 68" QUILT

These are unfinished block sizes. Note that some sizes do not need the 1/2"!

Block	Fabric(s)	Size(")	Number
A	Layer Cake squares or various focus prints	10" x 10"	12
B	Pieced rail fence blocks - *Various prints and solids*	10" x 10"	11
C	Half Size Blocks *Improvisationally pieced blocks—various prints and solids*	10" x 5¼"	4
D	Improvisationally pieced blocks— *various prints and solids*	3½" x 4½"	30
E	Border Block *Background fabric*	4½" x 58.5"	1
F	Border Block *Background fabric*	2½" x 58.5"	2
G	Border Block *Background fabric*	3½" x 48"	2
H	Border Block *Background fabric*	5½" x 48"	1
I	Border Block *Background fabric*	7" x 58.5"	1

LAYER CAKES AND RAIL FENCE IMPROV QUILT

ASSEMBLY DIAGRAM: 48" x 53" QUILT

MADLY MODERN QUILTS

ASSEMBLY DIAGRAM: 58" x 68" QUILT

FINISHING AND BINDING

Assemble your quilt using the Assembly Diagram.

Layering, basting and quilting: Layer the quilt top, backing and batting. Baste and quilt as desired.

Binding: Bind the quilt using your preferred style.

LAYER CAKES AND RAIL FENCE IMPROV QUILT

PLANNING YOUR QUILT

Ready to start planning your own quilt? Copy the template on this page. Use colored pencils or cut small pieces of fabric and glue them down to see how the colors might work.

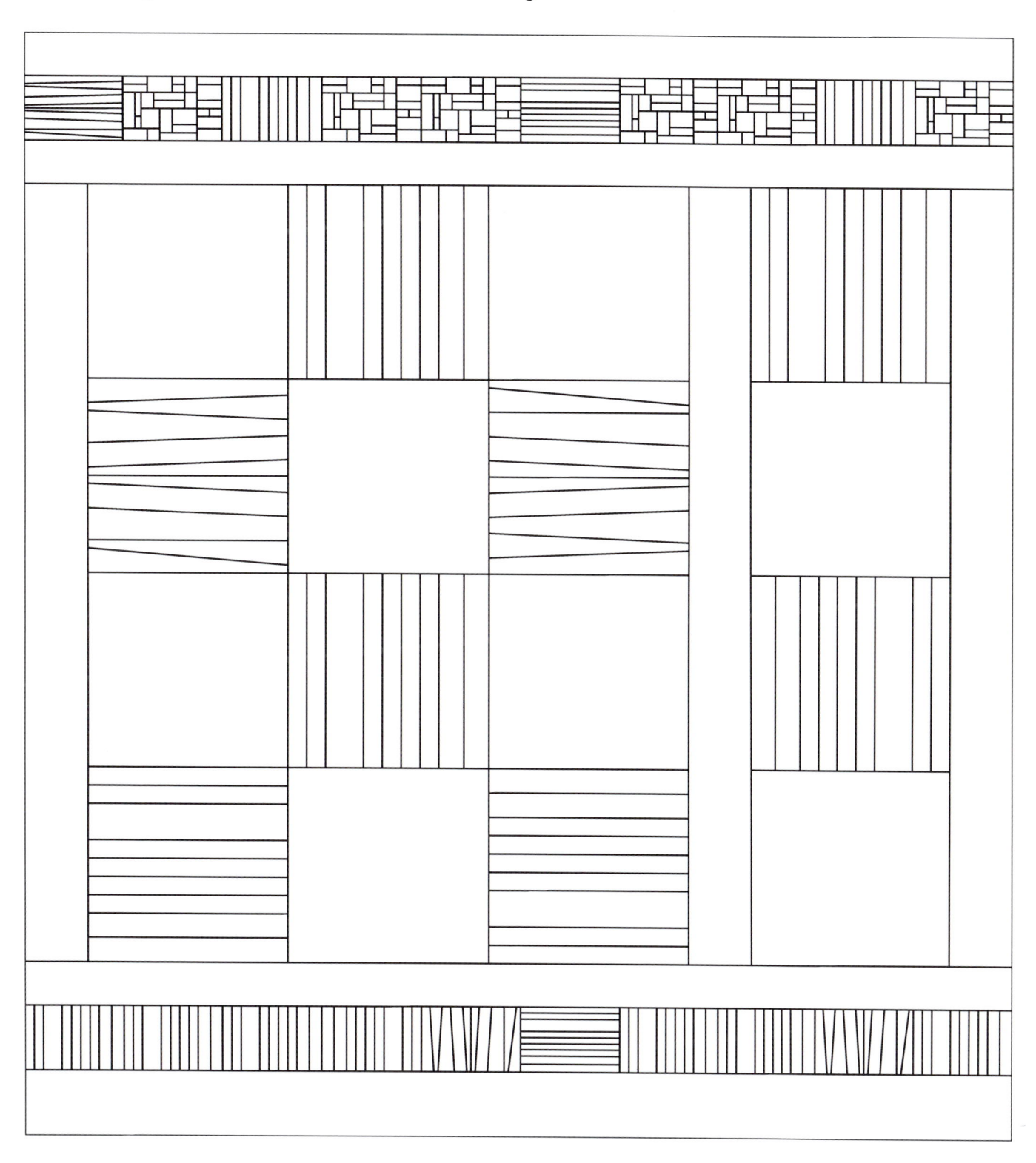

11 FLAMINGO MINI QUILT

FINISHED SIZE: 25" x 25"

FLAMINGO MINI QUILT

INTRODUCTION

This is a miniature version of the *Fractured Disappearing Nine Patch Quilt* and uses the same techniques on a smaller scale. Mini quilts make excellent swap items and can sometimes be made with scraps left over from a larger project.

You will use these modern quilting design elements:

› Asymmetry
› Modern traditionalism
› Using a modern color palette
› Improvisation

MATERIALS LIST

Fabric estimates are generous, allowing sufficient scraps to start piecing a coordinated backing.

You will need:

› Fat quarter or large scraps of bold modern print—this is your focus fabric. This fabric will serve as your color palette—check the selvedge dots for the colors that are in this print. If there is a central motif, like the flamingos in this quilt, be sure you can cut a 6½" square with the motif in the center.
› Fat eighth or large scraps of one coordinating print
› Fat eighths or large scraps of two to four coordinating solids
› Fat quarter of a geometric print or stripe
› 1¼ yard of your background fabric in a solid or near-solid for maximum contrast *(yellow in the sample)*

MADLY MODERN QUILTS

CUTTING TABLE

These are unfinished block sizes.

Block	Size	Fabric	Number
A	6½" x 6½"	Focus Fabric (center block of the quilt)	1
B	6½" x 6½"	Background Fabric	4
C	6½" x 6½"	Improvisationally pieced using various prints and solids	4
D	3½" x 18½"	Background Fabric	1
E	3½" x 21½"	Background Fabric	1
F	4½" x 21½"	Background Fabric	1
G	1½" x 25½"	Background Fabric	1
H	2½" x 12½"	Stripe or Print Fabric	1
I	2½" x 6½"	Background Fabric	1
J	2½" x 7½"	Background Fabric	1
K	2½" x 25½"	Background Fabric	1

INSTRUCTIONS

1. *Block A:* Cut one 6½" square so that it features your central motif.
2. *Block B:* Cut four 6½" squares from your background fabric.
3. *Block C:* Improvisationally piece four 6½" squares from your coordinating prints, solids and geometric or stripe. Have fun, don't over-think the process. See page 76 for piecing technique.
4. *Block H:* Cut Block H from your stripe or geometric print.
5. *Blocks D, E, F, G, I, J, K:* Cut these blocks from your background fabric

FREEFORM TIP: BLOCK H
You can improvisationally piece Block H instead of using a striped or geometric print.

COMPLETING THE TOP

1. Assemble the central nine patch from the A, B and C Blocks.
2. Sew Blocks D to the 9 Patch. This is now your central unit. Piece Blocks E and F to this unit.
3. Sew Block H to Blocks I and J.
4. Piece all remaining borders to complete the top.

FINISHING AND BINDING

Layering, basting and quilting: Layer the quilt top, backing and batting. Baste and quilt as desired.

Binding: Bind the quilt using your preferred style.

MAKING A HANGING SLEEVE

After you have quilted and bound the quilt, you can add a hanging sleeve. Cut a piece of fabric measuring 3" x 24". Turn all four raw edges under by 1/4 inch and iron. Hand sew the top of the sleeve to the top back of quilt.

BEFORE you sew the bottom of the sleeve, pin it so that you leave slack in it. Insert two fingers or the rod you will use before sewing the bottom of the sleeve. This will lift the sleeve slightly. Pin the bottom at this position. Hand sew the bottom of the sleeve onto the quilt. The slack allows you to insert a rod or slat comfortably without buckling the top of the quilt. In other words, don't make the sleeve tight against the back of the quilt.

FLAMINGO MINI QUILT

ASSEMBLY DIAGRAM

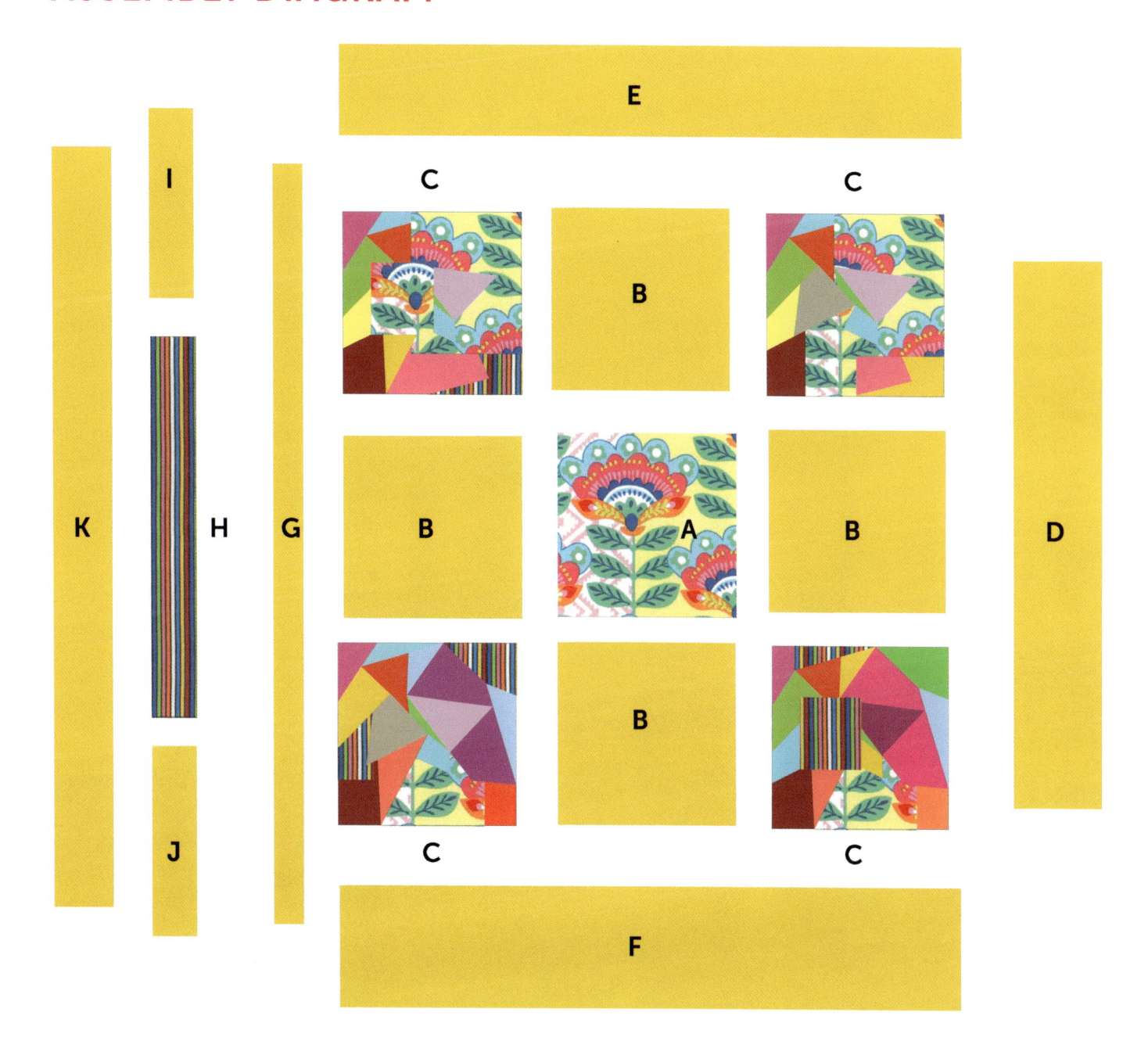

MADLY MODERN QUILTS

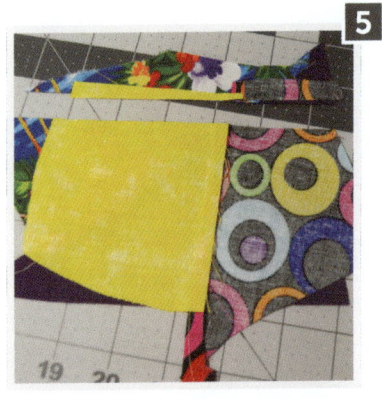

INSTRUCTIONS: PAPER BAG IMPROVISATION

Use the paper bag method for improvisational piecing Block C. I use this fun exercise in my workshops.

1. Put the fabrics you will use to make these blocks into a large brown paper bag. If you're using fat quarters, cut the fabric into pieces with scissors! No measuring! In Figure 1 you see a pile ready to go into the paper bag.

2. Reach into the bag without looking and pick two pieces of fabric at a time and find the longest sides that you can stitch together. In Figure 2 and 3, you see 3 pairs that I will now stitch together.

3. Sew the pairs together (Figure 4 and 5). don't worry that the pieces will not be the same length. That's OK--after all, you're just using up scraps.

4. Keep selecting and sewing until you have 8 or 10 pairs.

5. Sew pairs to other pairs to make a larger piece of fabric. You can cut pieces with scissors or a rotary cutter to make a straight edge to sew them together neatly (Figure 6). Keep cutting and adding onto these pieces until you have square-ish blocks measuring at least 7" on each side.

6. Cut off the sides (Figure 7).

7. Your final product will be a 6½" square, as seen in Figure 8.

8. If you need to make LARGER finished sizes, then keep sewing until your block is at least 1 inch or more larger than the size you need. Then go to step 5 (figure 7) and trim it to the size you need.

FLAMINGO MINI QUILT

Printed in Great Britain
by Amazon